Magister:

The Phenomenon of Mission and Camaraderie

Rogers-Freire for Social Justice.

The Story of the 5-Year Long Magister Institute Told by Former Cuban Jesuits.

Magister:

The Phenomenon of Mission and Camaraderie

Rogers-Freire for Social Justice.

---

*The Story of the 5-Year Long Magister Institute
Told by Former Cuban Jesuits.*

Jose R. Cruz, Ph.D.

To order additional copies of this book, contact:
Palibrio
1663 Liberty Drive
Suite 200
Bloomington, IN 47403
Toll Free from the U.S.A 877.407.5847
Toll Free from Mexico 01.800.288.2243
Toll Free from Spain 900.866.949
From other International locations +1.812.671.9757
Fax: 01.812.355.1576
orders@palibrio.com
726025

CONTENTS

Before you read the dissertation
Read its Final words:

Conclusions
Recommendations
Implications
Chapter Summary

Conclusions

The following conclusions are supported by the findings of this study. First, the set of characteristics described in the section A New Rogers-Freire-Goleman Paradigm of this study and attributed to the Magister Institute's leadership style were substantiated by the research participants in their interviews and post-interviews conversations and dialogues with the researcher. It should be pointed out that this MI's leadership style related only to the founding group of former Jesuits, and the study was not extended to include the complex and diverse entire 19-member group which incorporated at one time all the founding members' spouses, the new added non-Jesuit-related couples and single persons. There is one element to highlight as by-product of this detailed analysis, the perception by all the members that this was a "group or team of equals" or a "consensus management group." These two expressions seemed to convey in their minds that MI group reached the highest level of person-centeredness and attained an ideal form of personal and group consensus management.

Secondly, the short-term goal of collaboration with the Jesuits was challenged by one current Jesuit in his exposition and came out to be accepted by most of the group members once the real expectations of each were clearly exposed. This unanticipated discovery came about after a complete set of core elements of former Jesuit strivings was followed through until its furthest confines. The reasoned conception of Magister Institute included the following descriptions: "a group of equals"(MI-2, MI-3, and MI-4); "without organizational structure of any type" (MI-6, MI-3, MI-4, and MI-7); "with total flexibility"(MI-3) "our own, indigenous, home-grown, organizational framework and setting" (MI-6); and "a group endowed with efficacious solidarity to carry forward a vision of reality, in this case, Christian, Catholic, and within the Ignatian paradigm" (MI-7). Once these elements were grouped together and transformed into a vision, most of the members, starting with this researcher, accepted this new vision and emphasis as a new and more enriching goal and a substitute for the one of collaboration. The former Jesuits should have trusted in themselves and created a group based on their own personal experience. Things were supposed to be done at their own pace, under the light of their own lantern, and with their indigenous leadership style of supervision. Now the former Jesuits are able to trust in each other again and look at the Jesuits without awakening in themselves any negative feeling.

Thirdly, the method employed has shown its usefulness to study action groups in a short period of time. Once a researcher has a clear and precise idea of the methodology to be employed, and can bring to a core group of researchers persons involved in the activity in question, the use of open-ended interviews should provide the expected necessary information; of course the sample group must be selected among key persons in the life of the organization. Time and cost are two important factors to be considered when new efforts to re-orient health organizations, educational programs, and so many other service providers are urgently needed.

Fourthly, the comparison that some members made of the Magister Institute with the CLC and ACU's organizational and management styles was very enlightening and refreshing. Contradictions never explained before became understandable, and realities standing in the way were identified facilitating the pursuit of identity and mission as more viable alternatives.

Fifthly, the highlighted imbedded sense of mission of the founding members made their unity and common vision a viable alternative. MI-3 exclaimed with firmness and self-confidence: "our commitment to mission is not negotiable." This general perception of a profound and permanent bond established by former Jesuits with their sense of mission might be one of their most attractive characteristics when the values and possibilities of their collaboration are being considered.

There seems to be, also, good reason to sustain from the findings of this study that there are former Jesuits and former religious who will perceive as attractive and fulfilling collaborating with organizations and institutions of the Catholic Church.

Finally, this researcher made clear that the heuristic phenomenologic method employed to study this complex and intricate religious organization facilitated its global comprehension while shedding light to understand the uniqueness and otherness of several of its key components. This study analyzed and assessed the creation, development and leadership strategies of Magister Institute offering a global all-inclusive perspective while contributing to comprehend several core and separate elements of its standard operating style.

Recommendations

Further Research

A review of the literature reveals that there is little or no research done in the Spanish world concerning former Jesuit groups' creation and/ or development. Personal communication with historians connected to Jesuit studies revealed also that little or no known literature of this type is known to exist. It seems self-evident that this study fills a gap and may act as catalytic for other similar endeavors. This study however may contribute to the knowledge of an existing reality, the former Jesuits, the former religious and the non-active priests in search of a job in the area of their training and past experience. Other studies, whether quantitative or qualitative may contribute to further understand their situation and its significance to the Church and society.

Implications

Finally, this study has a methodological and theoretical background. It is also based in the lived experience of a group of people who have been part of the phenomenon to be studied, including the main researcher. The unique experience of the study not only has provided clarification of situations and ideas, but also the betterment of the quality of leadership in concrete organizations. Hopefully this kind of dissertation contributes also by providing guidelines to replicate similar studies and thus to better organizations, groups, and communities. Studies like this reach the group and the organization with its leaders and members. It touches through the written word the minds and hearts of future students interested in advancing the cause of the groups and organizations implicated in the studies. It also provides a methodological and theoretical foundation for the scientific apparatus indispensable in producing these results. Possibly interested readers will find not only theoretical and speculative challenges in this research but also a personal invitation to receive and carry forward this humble but proud academic and scientific torch.

Chapter Summary

This chapter presented a summary of the entire theoretical and methodological foundations of this study after the heuristic phenomenological research was conducted. The purpose of this study was presented together with a summary of the significance it will have in the areas of society connected with former Jesuits, former religious, non-active priests, and religious organizations or Church services. The importance of these former religious was emphasized and the value of this study for their current religious organizations was discussed. A brief presentation of the method and its limitations was offered and its implications discussed. The findings were presented in the form of themes, the product of the analysis of the different transcribed interviews. Six themes – camaraderie, the identity of Magister, the wives, attraction and mistrust, collaboration, and leadership style – were presented and carefully interrelated by providing direct information (quotations) from each of the seven research participants. A discussion of the findings was offered and a number of conclusions was submitted. Finally, some notes were presented on the state of research after this study and the implications for practice were highlighted. Finally the researcher invited the future researcher to continue the serious and hard work by receiving and carrying forward this humble but proud academic and scientific torch.

PREFACE

I have known Jose R. Cruz, Ph.D. for more than four decades. During these years I have had the opportunity to follow his career and watch his success in the fields of social change and social justice in Chicago, the Dominican Republic, and Miami. In this book, Dr. Cruz offers us the key to understanding this successful career. I have had the opportunity of being his partner, his colleague, his friend, and many times, his critic. In this book, Dr. Cruz demonstrates, once more that he continues to be one of the utmost experts in the thinking of Carl Rogers in Latin America.

As a Jesuit priest, Dr. Cruz was able to blend with ease and elegance the fire and critical pedagogical expertise of Paulo Freire, with Roger's humanistic person-centered psychology. Much to his credit, Dr. Cruz has taken the ground-breaking community psychology concepts of writers such as Rappaport and has raised them to a higher level, developing a synthesis with the Jesuit social justice values and the philosophy inspired by the Rev. Pedro Arrupe.

Today, Dr. Cruz is married, and his two children work with him in our Peter Pan Border Operation non-profit organization.

If you want to move forward in your understanding of social justice in the non-profit sector of society, read and critically study **From Rogers to Freire to Goleman Paradigm**. If you really want to know the truth, this paradigm should be called *Dr. Cruz' Paradigm of Social Justice*. This paradigm alone, as Sister Superfinski so eloquently stated, would have made this book truly **ground breaking**.

Jorge A. Herrera M.D., Ph.D.
President, Peter Pan Border Operation
Associate Professor of Psychiatry
Herbert Wertheim College of Medicine
Florida International University

The author brings a fresh and novel approach to the issue in question.

His methodology has been scrupulously developed and applied and his results are interesting and significant. I recommend it as an interesting contribution.

J.A. Solis-Silva, Ph.D.
Chair, Philosophy Department
St. John Vianney College Seminary.

Dr. Cruz and Phenomenological Heuristic Research

Dr. Eduardo Salvado, Sociologist

The German philosopher Immanuel Kant (1724-1804) was probably the most dominant philosopher after Aristotle (384-322). His Critique of Pure Reason" (1781) set in motion a major Paradigm Shift in global human thinking. Kant makes this question: Which ones are the necessary preconditions to have an objective human experience?

While Aristotle is interested in the "being as being", Kant is interested in "being as perceived by a social actor". This way, Kant provides a letter of citizenship to subjectivism in research. Kant makes a distinction between "noumenon" and "fenomenoun". The "noumenon" is reality in itself, and the "fenomenoun" is the reality as perceived by the social actor.

After Kant, all thinkers have tried to make reality objective. Thus, Edmund Husserl (1858-1938), the founder of "Phenomenology", is intent in providing objectivity to experience.

Cruz sails successfully, and in a superlative way, through the rough waters of the subjective-objective experiences of his five interviewees, founders of the "Magister Institute".

In his Dissertation's Chapter III, Cruz explains the methodology he will follow in his Research: "phenomenological heuristic research" about the creation, development and activities of the "Magister Institute".

Cruz successfully provides objectivity to the subjective perception of his interviewees. In Chapter IV the results of the Research are presented.

Doctor Sister Phyllis Superfisky And My Academic Work

These are the exact words describing the experience taking place between the former Jesuits and the "researcher" in the most graphic depiction of Magister.

Let this be our lasting expression so beautifully said in the song

"to Sir",

in this case, "to Sister with LOVE".

Jose R Cruz, PhD

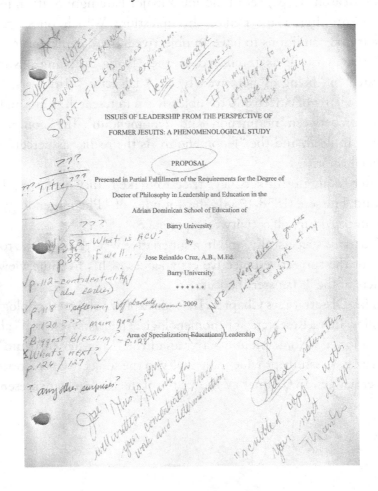

Rogers-Freire: A New Paradigm of Social Justice

Dr. Cruz has developed a new Freirian Paradigm of Critical Pedagogy. He has recreated Carl Rogers' Non-Directive/Person-Centered Psychotherapy, Counseling and Education's major concepts into a Joint Venture with Paulo Freire's Pedagogy of the Oppressed, as it appeared in Roger's chapter six of his book "Carl Rogers on Personal Power" (1977) entitled "The Person-Centered Approach and the oppressed". Rogers mentioned there that he has published "Freedom to Learn" in 1969 and that "Pedagogy of the Oppressed" was translated in 1969. Dr. Rogers clearly stated in the beginning of that famous chapter 6: "There is no indication that he had ever heard of my work, and I have never heard of his".

Dr. Rogers, in the second paragraph, of this mentioned chapter six, had this most beautiful and human passage about Paulo Freire:

> I was addressing students in educational institutions. He is telling about work with frightened, downtrodden peasants. I tried to use a style that would reach students and their teachers. He writes to communicate with Marxists.

Dr. Rogers makes a statement of the differences in their writing/ philosophical approach to teaching:

> I like to give concrete examples. He is almost completely abstract. Yet the principles he has come to build his work on are so completely similar to the principles of *Freedom to Learn* that I found myself open-mouthed with astonishment.

Let me raise my voice and appeal to all Person-Centered humanistic professionals to read this chapter two of Dr. Cruz's PhD dissertation and new book. Please, read "A New Rogers-Freire-Goleman Paradigm" and the entire work of Dr. Cruz, and appreciate Dr. Cruz's recreation of Paulo Freire's pioneer critical pedagogy.

I thank Fr. Román Espadas, S.J. for his intermediary gesture to make out encounters with Dr. Cruz possible in Havana Cuba: under the famous President Nydia Gonzalez's *mangueira* (Mango tree) surrounded by the Teachers/Pedagogues Association, Asociación de Pedagogos de Cuba (APC) honoring Paulo Freire. That day we were blessed with the presence of Nita Araujo Freire.

Fr. Roman also provided me with Cruz's original philosophical and pedagogic background: from Helder Cámara to Fr. Pedro Arrupe to ROGERS to FREIRE to Goizueta to Pope Francis.

As Nita Araujo Freire said to all the participants of the encyclopedic and ground-breaking volume of *Critical Pedagogy* (2007), in the Advance Praise section:

> "Like Paulo Freire" and Cruz, I dare to add, "they propose that we recapture and safeguard the greatest patrimony that justifies and gives meaning to life itself: our humanity."

Professor Mariano Alberto Isla Guerra
Doctor in Pedagogical Sciences
Executive National Board Member
Pedagogues Association of Cuba (APC)

To Rev. Roman Espadas, S.J.
One "estudioso" of Paulo Freire and enthusiastic promoter of his movement.

To Nita Freire, the heart and soul of Paulo Freire's presence

To all those whose MISSION is social change and social justice

ISSUES OF LEADERSHIP FROM THE PERSPECTIVE OF
FORMER JESUITS: A PHENOMENOLOGICAL STUDY

DISSERTATION

Presented in Partial Fulfillment of the Requirements for the Degree of

Doctor of Philosophy in Leadership and Education in the

Adrian Dominican School of Education of

Barry University

by

Jose Reinaldo Cruz, A.B., M.Ed.

Barry University

* * * * * *

2009

Area of Specialization: Educational Leadership

ISSUES OF LEADERSHIP FROM THE PERSPECTIVE OF

FORMER JESUITS: A PHENOMENOLOGICAL STUDY

DISSERTATION

by

Jose Reinaldo Cruz

2009

APPROVED BY:

Sister Phyllis Superfisky, SFCC, Ph.D.
Chairperson, Dissertation Committee

Alicia Marill, D.Min.
Member, Dissertation Committee

John G. Dezek, Ed.D.
Member, Dissertation Committee

Terry Piper, Ph.D.
Dean, Adrian Dominican School of Education

ABSTRACT

ISSUES OF LEADERSHIP FROM THE PERSPECTIVE OF
FORMER JESUITS: A PHENOMENOLOGICAL STUDY
Jose Reinaldo Cruz
Barry University. 2009
Dissertation Chairperson: Sister Phyllis Superfisky, SFCC, Ph.D.

Purpose. This study, based mostly on individual interviews and dialogues, examined the leadership styles and other significant experiences of ten former Jesuits connected with the foundation of the Magister Institute, in Miami, Florida.

Method. The research methods and strategies were founded on the qualitative tradition of inquiry as they are interpreted and refined by the phenomenological heuristic research model. A six-step process followed the completion of the collection of the data. The six steps are as follows: Initial engagement, Immersion into the topic and question, Incubation, Illumination, Explication, and Creative synthesis. All of these steps are interconnected by means of dialogue.

A special effort of comparing and sharing the opinions of the founding members, a true process of triangulation and member checking, functioned as a guarantee of the rigor and trustworthiness of the study (Moustakas, 1994). The researcher was nondirective and permissive in the dialogues and interviews.

Major Findings. First, the set of characteristics described in the section A New Rogers-Freire-Goleman Paradigm of this study and attributed to the Magister Institute's leadership style were substantiated by the research participants in their interviews and post-interviews conversations and dialogues with the researcher. It was the unanimous perception of all the members that this was a "group or team of equals" or a "consensus management group." These two expressions seemed to convey in their minds that MI group reached the highest level of person-centeredness and attained an ideal form of personal and group consensus management. Secondly, the short-term goal of collaboration with the S. J. was challenged and a new concept of relationship with the Jesuits was embraced by most of the group members. Thirdly, the method employed has shown its usefulness to study action groups in a short period of time. Time and cost are two factors recommending this method. Fourthly, the highlighted imbedded sense of mission of the founding members made their unity and common vision a viable alternative. Finally, the heuristic phenomenologic method employed to study this complex and intricate religious organization facilitated its global comprehension while shedding light to understand the uniqueness and otherness of several of its key components.

CHAPTER I

THE PROBLEM

Introduction

This is a study of the leadership style embedded in the creation and development of the Magister Institute. The Magister Institute is an official member of the Christian Life Community, the largest worldwide lay group associated with the Society of Jesus (S.J.). This Institute was initiated in 2004 in Miami-Dade County by ten former Jesuits of the Antilles Province of the Society of Jesus who first gathered socially at the invitation of one of the former Jesuits and priests to discuss the possibility of sharing in common apostolic work. In time, this unstructured group of former Jesuits, assisted by appropriate leadership strategies, moved from being distant and separate from the Jesuits to becoming their collaborators. The minutes, reflections, and assembled materials of the Magister Institute's collected papers from 2004-2009 highlight some important moments of the progress of these former Jesuits as they developed into a vibrant group affiliated with the Christian Life Communities. The study explored the leadership processes that guided these men in their sincere search for their roots, identity, and a reoriented mission in life.

This study is a qualitative investigation of the impact of the Executive Committee's (EC) leadership style and other group processes leading to the creation and development of the Magister Institute. It is hoped that, at a time when so many members leave their religious organizations within the Catholic Church, this study can be of interest to religious organizations who seek to understand the journey of members who leave. This study also showed how, with appropriate leadership, former members can provide services to religious organizations, parishes, and communities and help reduce the workload on overburdened religious and priestly personnel (Magister Institute Collected Papers, 2004-2008; McDonough & Bianchi, 2002).

Statement of the Problem

This study examined the leadership styles and other significant lived experiences connected with the foundation of the Magister Institute, an official member of the Christian Life Community. Most of the members of the original group of ten former Jesuits went through various transitional stages: first, a process of the initial struggle of separation and distancing themselves from the Society of Jesus; second, living and working disconnected from the Jesuits over a period of several years; and finally, after much emotional deliberation, re-approaching the Society of Jesus, the Jesuits, for some form of working realignment through the creation and development of the Magister Institute (Magister Institute Collected Papers, 2004-2008).

The leadership styles of the Executive Committee of the Magister Institute used in the initial meetings and throughout its foundation and development were examined. Its impact on the overall effectiveness of its strategies were also assessed and analyzed. This study was based on the descriptions provided in five long and two short interviews by a selected group of research participants interrelated through the Magister Institute. These interviews were open-ended based on the main research questions leading this investigation. Carefully designed nondirective open-ended subquestions were also used appropriately to assure the quality and comprehensiveness of the depictions from each interview. These descriptions were analyzed following heuristic-phenomenologic methodological strategies based on the studies and writings of Moustakas (1990, 1994). The relevance of the theological and philosophical paradigm of the Magister Institute, an official member of the Christian Life Community was also described and analyzed (Magister Institute, Letter of Acceptance, 2005).

The study was focused on the accurate description, analysis, and interpretation of the lived experiences and successful leadership processes of the members of the Magister Institute. The role of the researcher, who is also a member of the Executive Committee of the group and carries with them major responsibility for its leadership style, was critically evaluated in its role in facilitating the development of this heuristic-phenomenological research. The researcher's role as a member of the Executive Committee of the group being investigated was key in this study's effort to combine participant observations and heuristic-phenomenological research. According to Moustakas (1990, 1994), heuristic phenomenology emphasizes direct involvement of researcher and participants and continued dialogue and interaction not only before but especially during and after conducting the research.

This qualitative study concentrated on the leadership and other processes of the former Jesuits, within the context of the Magister Institute they formed. This heuristic-phenomenologic study first touched upon the history of the leadership style and the shared culture of the members of the Magister Institute. Second, this research respectfully described the behaviors, opinions, and interpretations of several members of the Jesuit community who played a key role in the collaboration of the former Jesuits with current members of the Society of Jesus. The study gathered two kinds of observations: emic (views of the research participants, informants, and others), and etic (views of the main researcher). Since the researcher is also a participant observer, his observations and insights on the phenomenon under scrutiny were carefully considered and respected for their inherent value, and for the knowledge stemming from the processes of triangulation and continuous feedback with the research participants.

Purpose of the Study

This study was designed to explore the transition of ten Jesuits who broke away from their religious organization and, after several years of individual isolation from the Society of Jesus, transitioned to a coherent group. The experience of the group led them eventually to approach the Jesuit organization and to make a formal proposal to rejoin them in their apostolic activities as official associates (Christian Life Communities). Considering that the experiences they expressed in the initial and following reunions seemed to be so emotionally deep (Magister Institute collected papers, 2004-2005), this story has surfaced several compelling dimensions including those of human interest and curiosity. A non expected form of conciliatory ending of such a story is ground breaking, considering that the majority of this informal group of friends, especially the very vocal ones, initially stubbornly resisted having any self-initiated dialogue with the Jesuits.

When these former Jesuits gathered to become a group, to share their life experiences, to deal with their past feelings and present readjustments, it was extremely emotional and full of conflict. The group, since the earliest draft of its "Estatutos Generales" (Magister Institute collected papers, 2004-2005) also required selecting coordinators. Above all, the success of the process would have to be a function of a different kind of leadership. In their early meetings, several outspoken members threatened to leave the unstructured gatherings rather than talk about becoming a more formal group, or even approaching the Jesuits. The other members listened to these objections in silence and respect because most of them had suffered a great deal (Magister Institute collected papers, first meeting, 2004-2005). This group was quickly becoming a more cohesive unit and needed to move on promptly to avoid the risk of disintegrating and dissolving (Napier & Gershenfeld, 2004). At that juncture, a member of this group upheld a determined, incipient, and vague idea of pulling together all of these talented individuals with patience and enthusiasm to do some kind of apostolic work (Magister

MAGISTER: THE PHENOMENON OF MISSION AND
CAMARADERIE ROGERS-FREIRE FOR SOCIAL JUSTICE.

29

Institute collected papers, members' reflections, 2005). Most of the members thought it undignified and inappropriate to approach the Jesuits with any kind of proposal. The Executive Committee selected to lead this former Jesuit group had to contend with three PhDs, five former Jesuits and priests, a leading educator, and a litigation attorney. Coordinating this group was a daunting challenge (Magister Institute collected papers, 2008). These ten individuals were adamant about protecting their freedom from any outside interference and had moving stories to relate concerning their lives within the Jesuit Order. They made no attempts to question, dispute, or judge each other out of respect and understanding of the hurtful circumstances most of them seemed to have experienced. Nevertheless, after about two hours of discussion at their first meeting, there was a consensus that the group was ready to consider some meaningful apostolic work. At their third meeting in 2004, a notable milestone was reached when the group agreed on general operating principles, a mission, and to call themselves the "Magister Institute."

The purpose of this research, first and foremost, was to describe and examine the leadership strategies guiding this group in its process of self-discovery and reconciliation. Second, this study documented and analyzed some of the individual feelings expressed, unrealized hopes, feelings of separation and at times isolation. This examination described the personal quest for intimacy and personal autonomy, hopes for changes in structural social justice that could now be difficult to achieve, numerous pains both disclosed or yet to surface, and some of the never-ending nostalgia for those same-age friends in each of their former Jesuit communities (Magister Institute collected papers, 2004-2009; McDonough & Bianchi, 2002).

This study was based on written information collected in the archives of the Magister Institute. This investigation utilized mostly individual interviews and dialogues to explore the phenomenon and described and explored the leadership styles of these individuals and their feelings, emotions, and ideas leading to the creation and establishment of the Magister Institute. The objective was to analyze and synthesize the individual depictions of the inception of the group in its process of becoming the Magister Institute up to the time of its split into two distinct organizations. The researcher integrated all of these descriptions and formulated a composite, comprehensive depiction.

The number of former religious men and women of the Catholic Church has been growing over the last 40 years. The situation of the Jesuits, the largest religious organization of the Catholic Church in the world, and also the largest religious organization of the Catholic Church in the United States, is extremely dramatic: there are more former Jesuits than current Jesuits in the United States at the present time (McDonough & Bianchi, 2002). In the experience of this group, former religious, men and women may find not only understanding of their own personal situations, but also inspiration to strive for identity and mission in life. Hopefully, the Catholic Church's hierarchy will find these "born-again" religious men and women prepared and appropriately fitted for the challenges currently facing the Church. The Catholic Church is undergoing serious crises in the public perception of the celibate priesthood and the scarcity of personnel at all levels of commitment in their ranks. If former religious and priests could join their overworked and overwhelmed peers currently active in religious and priestly service, they could make a significant contribution to the different Catholic communities of the Church. This study will offer leading guidelines and interpretation of the processes these men experienced. Thousands of similar men and women, and numerous dioceses and religious congregations around the world could benefit from this research.

A final reason justifying this study is that there is no serious or trustworthy literature on Latin American former Jesuits (Saez, S.J., personal communication, 2009). There is nothing in the literature about any former Jesuits gathering themselves into a group that has been accepted to work with the Jesuits as associates. This study is the first of its kind and hopefully will encourage other researchers to continue in a similar fashion and enhance the understanding of the leadership styles, descriptions, analyses, and interpretations of the shared culture of this group of former Jesuits.

Background

The group of former Jesuits who met and decided to discuss the possibilities of engaging in some kind of apostolic work in common was originally made up of ten men, all of them originally from Cuba, and ranging in ages from 50 to 67. They all knew most of the former and current Jesuits of the Society of Jesus associated with the Antilles Province (Dominican Republic, Cuba, Puerto Rico and Miami-Dade County, Florida, U.S.A.). Several of them were close friends and classmates. They all spoke English fluently, though their language used among themselves was always Spanish. Actually, Spanish was the official language of the group and all original documents were written in Spanish.

Since the Society of Jesus is considered one of the first-rate, largest, and highly educated religious organizations of the Catholic Church (McDonough, 1998), the study is expected to provide understanding and knowledge of the processes involved in the difficult, sensitive, and common transitions of religious members leaving their organizations.

The study has relied solely on the depictions of the active participants of this research, namely, five former Jesuits, and the clarifications and opinions of two current members of the Society of Jesus of the Antilles Province. The founders of the Magister Institute were six of the original number of ten former Jesuits who participated in the first three meetings. One of these six members is not presently in the State of Florida and communication with him was considered impractical (Magister Institute collected papers, 2004-2009).

It is hoped that a substantial portion of the Catholic community interested in the religious and intellectual development of the contemporary Church as well as leaders of religious congregations will benefit from this research.

The original group of the Magister Institute accepted new members of both genders who were aligned with the Institute's work and philosophy, grew in strength to 19 members, and subsequently broke up into two groups. Only one of these two groups is heir to the name "Magister Institute," though both groups continue to be associated officially with the Jesuit Order through their membership in the Christian Life Community.

Research Question

In qualitative research, focus and purpose are kept on target by a well-structured overarching research question. This understanding is generally accepted by all qualitative research traditions of inquiry (Creswell, 1998). The overarching questions served to direct and focus the interviews and related conversations during the entire process of the data collection and analysis, and finally, facilitated the necessary consensus for the final creative synthesis of the writing process.

The heuristic-phenomenological approach adopted in this study (Moustakas, 1990, 1994; Creswell, 1998) required a dialogic method and general attitude on the part of the main researcher in his relationship with research participants. This new leadership style has been such that the interviews and conversations with research participants looked more like a dialogue, an empathic mutual understanding, and a person-centered human interaction (Moustakas, 1990). The subquestions following the main overarching questions were actually meant to be understood in this light.

The overarching research questions were as follows:

What are your recollections/perceptions of your lived experiences in the creation and development of the Magister Institute?

What are your recollections/perceptions of the leadership style of the Executive Committee in the creation and development of the Magister Institute?

The following subquestions were presented as a stimulus and inspiration to help each research participant accurately describe a

MAGISTER: THE PHENOMENON OF MISSION AND
CAMARADERIE ROGERS-FREIRE FOR SOCIAL JUSTICE.

33

more comprehensive depiction of the phenomenon under scrutiny: the leadership style and processes including other personal and group experiences leading to the creation and development of the Magister Institute (Magister Institute collected papers, 2004-2009).

1. What, in your own words, are all the aspects of your feelings of separation from the Society of Jesus, as well as the experiences you have encountered with the religious and lay administrations of the Catholic Church?

2. What were the leadership strategies and any other ideas, feelings or emotions connected with the Society of Jesus that you consider most influential in the consolidation of the Magister Institute?

3. What were your fears and hopes for re-association with the Jesuits? What connection do you see between the leadership style of the Executive Committee and the reduction of your fears?

4. With the degree of success attained in the re-association of the former Jesuits of the Magister Institute with the current Jesuits in the Antilles Province, how much of this accomplishment do you think is related to the leadership style of members of the Magister Institute?

5. What do you think are the possibilities of success of similar alternatives elsewhere in the Catholic Church? Given your experience at the Magister Institute, and the scarcity of Jesuits, what do you think of the interest shown by the Society of Jesus in re-associating with the former Jesuits to provide apostolic work? What are your thoughts about the degree and kind of re-association achieved between the current Jesuits of Miami, Florida, U.S.A., Dominican Republic, and Cuba, called the Antilles Province of the Society of Jesus, and the former Jesuits of the Magister Institute?

This is a study that has offered key guidelines in a phenomenological description of the personal experiences and observations of these men. The researcher selected five members of the Magister Institute, including himself, and two current Jesuits, all of them with direct lived experiences related to the development of the Magister Institute. Heuristic phenomenological research strategies helped to understand what each participant in the research described as part of the experience of the "phenomenon" depicted, that is, the leadership style of the Executive Committee and the development of the Magister Institute, its purpose, achievements, and all related experiences connected with it.

Theoretical Framework

The theories and explanations that guided this research study are the following:

1. The heuristic-phenomenologic approach facilitated understanding of the description of the phenomenon under scrutiny, that is, the establishment and development of the Magister Institute and the General Principles of the Christian Life Communities, as adopted and adapted by the Magister Institute in its General Principles and General Statutes (Magister Institute collected papers, 2009; Moustakas, 1990, 1994).

2. The person-centered, non-directive approach to leadership of Carl Rogers that is related to the permissive and open atmosphere, free from fears and authoritarian impositions, supposedly characteristic of the leadership strategies of the Magister Institute and its government-by-consensus as the ordinary way of proceeding (Kahn, 1999; Rogers, 1961, 1970, 1977).

3. The critical pedagogy and social analysis of reality of Paulo Freire is directly related to the understanding and interpretation of the main three characteristics of the Magister Institute's formative philosophy: the critical form of social analysis, the discernment of spirits, and the preferential option for the poor (Freire, 1969; Magister Institute Collected Papers, 2009; Iparraguirre, 1963).

MAGISTER: THE PHENOMENON OF MISSION AND
CAMARADERIE ROGERS-FREIRE FOR SOCIAL JUSTICE.

35

These main theoretical guidelines, together with the philosophical framework, constituted this dissertation's interpretive paradigm. The Magister Institute's development took place within Catholic/Jesuit theological, philosophical, and apostolic guidelines. These guidelines were sometimes an expression, mixed with feelings of ambiguity of the old ways vividly experienced by each one of the ten former Jesuits. At other times, this theoretical and practical collection of rules, desiderata, apostolate visions, and concrete behavioral and intellectual expectations were the latest, genuine expression of these former Jesuits in their quest for a unique mission and identity of their own. The integration of these two dimensional frameworks constituted the real interpretive paradigm of the experiences of the former Jesuits, now regrouped as the Magister Institute.

Significance of the Study

A group of Catholic Latin Caribbean men joined a rigorous religious organization and after varying periods of membership decided to notify their superiors and leave the organization at different stages of their religious lives. While their permission to separate from the Jesuit Order and their legal status in the Catholic Church was in process, these former Jesuits, five of whom were ordained priests, gathered to form the Magister Institute with the intention of becoming full-fledged members of the Archdiocese of Miami and coworkers and real associates of today's religious organizations, the same religious organizations of which they were former members. This investigation was necessary because it studied an unprecedented event in the history of the Catholic Church, namely, the tentative reacceptance of ten former Jesuits including five priests as a group they called the Magister Institute an official member of the Christian Life Communities.

The study described and analyzed the group members' perceptions of processes of culture sharing and leadership style through interviews, journals, letters, and other personal documents as they strove to reestablish their roots, identity, and mission in life. A culture-sharing phenomenological-heuristic study of this group of former Jesuits in their quest for personal and group identity and mission in life has elicited new insights into religious/ethnic processes involved in similar separation-reassociation research studies and the successful leadership styles that guide them.

The general public has perceived a serious crisis in the Catholic Church, besides the unethical behavior of some priests, particularly in the areas of priestly celibacy and scarcity of religious personnel to staff and serve in the institutions of the Church. It is conceivable that the ten former Jesuits, five of them priests, who were the focus of the study, might eventually be willing to make a significant contribution to many Catholic communities if they could, in some way, be allowed to participate alongside their former peers in their religious and priestly apostolic work.

The Jesuit Order, formally called the Society of Jesus (S.J.), is a Catholic organization founded by Pope Paul III in 1540 at the insistence of the then Inigo de Loyola, later known as St. Ignatius of Loyola, who, from a courtly gentleman became a hermit and then a deeply religious man, imbued with ideals of helping a Church that was in need of reform. Through their religious commitment of the three vows of poverty, chastity, and obedience, and from 10 to 14 years of philosophical and theological studies, the Jesuits form and rely on personal attachments among themselves. They are assigned to and perform various types of works such as teaching in schools and universities, doing scientific research, providing religious services and preaching at parishes, and promoting social justice and the advancement of the poor.

Within the Catholic Church, priests and religious who have separated themselves from their ministries or official religious organizations have traditionally remained distant from their former religious communities (McDonough & Bianchi, 2002). Today, nevertheless, there seems to be a growing tendency towards more understanding. Some recent related cases could be considered a slight indication of new trends pointing in the direction of a long-range true reconciliation (Magister Institute collected papers, 2004-2009).

The case of these ten former Jesuits is thought provoking. It includes a positive trend towards a future enriching re-association with a traditional religious institution and a break with its historic rigidity. This statement was challenged by the facts surfaced by the phenomenological analysis of interviews, letters, notes, and other relevant material collected in this research. This study has offered new insight into the leadership style and phenomenological processes involved in the life transitions of these ten men.

Actually not all of the ten former Jesuits considered their collaboration with the current members of the Society of Jesus an act of true reconciliation. At first glance, the true perception of the group of former Jesuits did not appear to be evident with the scarce information gathered in the collected papers of the Magister Institute. Clarification of these components, relationships, and their meaning was one of the main goals of the research.

This study focused on the narrative descriptions—interviews (approximately an hour each) and conversations (of up to twenty minutes)—of the lived experiences of each participant-observer chosen to be part of the sample. Their comprehensive descriptions were further elucidated through the help of documents, letters, notes, and any other personal records. The study was focused solely on the descriptions of the life experiences, narrated in a live and phenomenologically accurate way by the members of the research sample. Every effort was made not to add any foreign interpretation to the co-researchers' individual vivid comprehensive narrations and their resulting depictions (Moustakas, 1994). These depictions also involved phenomenological processes of a journey of a desired re-association and reconciliation. The conduct of this study required a very open and acceptant attitude on the part of the researcher, allowing the co-researchers to express their feelings and emotions about the creation of the Magister Institute, the sensitive stories of their breakaway from the Jesuits, and in some cases, their second breakaway, this time between those who remained in the original Magister Institute and those who created a new Christian Life Community.

The interviews and other exchanges of information between the main researcher and the participants were focused on the depictions obtained from each of the research participants.

Origins of Researcher's Interest in the Topic

The researcher of this study is a former Jesuit and Catholic priest. He was a Jesuit for 23 years. The last nine years of his Jesuit life were the first nine years of his priesthood. When analyzing a style of life one has always loved and been devoted to, looking at it in the past, the feelings and emotions tend to make descriptions and interpretations difficult.

The researcher of this study has written over 20 professional papers and has presented them at university symposia and other professional gatherings, including the conventions of the Dominican Association of Psychologists, and the international conventions of psychologists in Santo Domingo, Caracas, and Havana. He was also invited to present an exposition of the Master's Degree Program in Community Psychology he founded in Santo Domingo at the national convention of the American Psychological Association in Washington, D.C. (Cruz, 2009). These presentations were based in the applications of theories from Carl Rogers and Paulo Freire to community, education, and academic programs. This background and progressive development led him to pursue the Ph.D. program in Educational Leadership and to a dissertation following these two authors' theoretical frameworks.

The researcher and member of the Executive Committee of the group left the Jesuit religious organization without personal friction, continued in good standing with most current Jesuits, and was offered positions of leadership in schools run by the Jesuits, both in Santo Domingo and in Miami (Magister Institute collected papers, 2004-2008).

The origins of the researcher's interest in this topic have to do also with his proficiency in qualitative research and his involvement in this unique experience with the group of former Jesuits. His leadership position in the group, as its one of the key organizers and planners, made him very conscious of his role as one of the group of initiating

members. The other members of the group slowly realized that this
(becoming a member of the CLC community) was going to be an
invitation to associate with the Jesuits again, a kind of occurrence
they were unable to even dream about. Once the events unfolded, the
researcher and the other members of the Executive Committee realized
that they needed to prepare themselves for these positions of leadership.
They knew they needed to describe, analyze, and interpret the shared
culture of the group in order to understand it better and help facilitate
its development and maturity as a group at the crossroads of religion,
modernity, and social action (Creswell, 1998; Denzin & Lincoln, 1998;
Magister Institute members' reflections).

Research Design

The decision to use a qualitative research approach is based on the
characteristics of the problem to be studied and the kind of perspective
or understanding required from the investigation (Creswell, 2005). This
research study was concerned with a group of former religious men who
decided to "go back" to their former colleagues and negotiate working in
a group as associates and called the Magister Institute, a member of the
CLC. This type of group is very rare, and this collaboration extremely
uncommon, considering that it is the Society of Jesus with whom they
are attempting to re-associate. There is also a lack of literature on the
specific issue. The importance of forming groups similar to Magister
Institute is warranted. Given the scarcity of literature on this subject,
and the necessity of obtaining detailed information on issues related
to this organization that are very personal and subjective requiring
a non-objective approach, the recommended research paradigm to
study this unique and central phenomenon was qualitative research
(Creswell, 1998, 2005; Moustakas, 1990, 1994). The kind of knowledge
required was very personal, could only be obtained by listening to those
involved, and had to be requested through respectful, general, open-
ended questions. The knowledge of the group's creation, development,
and function, which will help other similar groups and ultimately

benefit members of the Church, had to be comprehensive and very detailed. Qualitative research methods, according to Creswell (2005) and Moustakas (1998, 1994), are best suited to study phenomena about which there is very limited information, and about which elaborate, critical, and comprehensive knowledge is required. There was a need to obtain personal knowledge from a group of former Jesuits, and to understand their perceptions of different events related to the foundation and development of the group they formed to work as associates (through the CLC membership) to the Jesuits of the Antilles Province. This kind of knowledge and the strategies to obtain it, such as interviews, dialogues, documents, were all part of the qualitative phenomenologic and heuristic repertoire. The qualitative researcher sought the truths in the phenomena mediated through perceptions of persons with direct access to them. These perceptions were part of descriptions and ultimately came down to themes and words—the live data of heuristic-phenomenologic research (Strauss & Corbin, 1998). Heuristic phenomenologic strategies are specially suited to study this kind of phenomenon.

Definition of Terms

A.C.U. The term stands for *Agrupación Católica Universitaria*. This is a Catholic organization associated with the Society of Jesus, called Sodality. The Sodalities were the precursors of the Christian Life Communities.

Christian Life Community (CVX). The term stands for a religious and Catholic lay organization based in Rome, officially associated with the Jesuits, and with a theological and philosophical paradigm expressed in their General Principles and By-Laws (Christian Life Community, 1991).

Ex-Jesuit. It is the term used for a former member of the Jesuit Order, who finished his novitiate, professed the three vows of Poverty, Chastity,

MAGISTER: THE PHENOMENON OF MISSION AND
CAMARADERIE ROGERS-FREIRE FOR SOCIAL JUSTICE.

41

and Obedience, and left the Jesuit Religious Order, with or without obtaining the proper permissions and dispensations (Iparraguirre, 1963). The founding members of Magister Institute requested to be called former Jesuits "antiguos Jesuitas" (Magister Institute collected papers, 2004-2009).

Jesuit. A Jesuit is a member of the Society of Jesus (S.J.), normally a Priest, Scholastic, or Brother (Iparraguirre, 1963).

Magister Institute (MI). Name used by the ten former Jesuit participants of this study for their group which became a member of the Christian Life Community (Magister Institute collected papers, 2004-2009).

Member checking. Process whereby the researcher shares his own interpretations and depictions with the research participants, thus clarifying possible misunderstandings. Normal areas of testing with the informants are data, categories of critical reflection, interpretations, and results (Johnson, 1997; Krefting, 1991).

Priest. An ordained minister of the Catholic Church in the rank of Priesthood, and the official Minister of the Eucharist (Mass) and of the Sacrament of Penance (Iparraguirre, 1963).

Reflexivity. Quality by which researchers use critical thinking and self-reflection throughout a study (Johnson, 1997).

Religious Order. An official organization of men or women who are bound by three permanent religious vows of Poverty, Chastity, and Obedience, and who are officially recognized as vowed religious by the Catholic Church (Iparraguirre, 1963).

Saint Ignatius of Loyola. Saint originally known as Inigo, from Spain who founded the Society of Jesus, and initiated the retreat method guided by the Spiritual Exercises (Iparraguirre, 1963).

Society of Jesus (S.J.). Religious organization of the Roman Catholic Church founded by Saint Ignatius of Loyola in the 16th century (Iparraguirre, 1963).

Spiritual Exercises. A very detailed manual for the conduction of the Jesuit method of spiritual retreat which is usually one to four weeks long and geared towards personal conversion, religious growth, and apostolic commitment (Iparraguirre, 1963).

Trustworthiness. Term replacing validity for use in qualitative research and made up of four aspects: truth value, applicability, consistency, and neutrality. These aspects are called the new criteria of trustworthiness (Denzin & Lincoln, 1999; Creswell, 1998; Krefting, 1991).

Limitations of the Study

Phenomenological-heuristic research requires a constant engagement of the researcher in the central phenomenon and with the research participants (Moustakas, 1994). The researcher, in his incessant dialogue with all participant-observers, increases his knowledge of the phenomenon under investigation, and simultaneously experiences creative self-discovery. This subjective involvement of the researcher makes his experience rich and unique and gives him a very special vantage point from which to describe and communicate his allocated depiction (Moustakas). The relationship between the researcher and the participant is one of closeness and mutual reciprocity. Only the researcher will perform the collection of data, codification, and theme finding. This may have the implication of bias and possible lack of objectivity. If handled properly, it could also mean one more witness offering a different and not necessarily partial viewpoint and depiction. On the other side, if the researcher respects the participants' point of view and privileged depiction, the consistency afforded by the researcher should increase the internal validity of the investigation. The research becomes more credible, that is to say, it brings out more truth to the descriptions of the phenomenon from one extra participant-observer from a privileged position. Although very personal and even passionate, it completes the description of the phenomenon from a non-biased point of view. The level of reflexivity of the researcher, accepting the possibility of his own personal bias, would help to make his professional participation trustworthy. This trustworthiness will be increased by the researcher showing knowledge and expertise in the non-directive and person-centered approach followed by him not only in his role as founding member of the Magister Institute but also now as the only researcher of this investigation.

A second limitation of this study rests on the ability and willingness of the group members to provide truthful and voluntary information in the interviews. The depiction of each interview itself could be tested by comparing it with other members' interview descriptions, that is, by triangulating it. The use of documents and dialogues served as another instance of multiple data source, and this was one of the core triangulation processes with focus on the interviews. The fact that the researcher followed a non-directive style of leadership (facilitator) as member of the Executive Committee of the group points in the direction of open-door kind of communication between the members and the Executive Committee.

These limitations and possible biases are part of the reality of weaknesses faced and dealt with in this investigation. Through a process of reflexivity (Milinki, 1999), these instances of limitation may be turned into assets and key evolving processes, making credibility and trustworthiness, the pillars of the validity structure, acceptable and scientifically plausible (Lincoln & Guba, 1985; Patton, 2002).

Chapter Summary

This chapter dealt with the purpose of the research, describing the leadership strategies of the Executive Committee of Magister Institute and all other meaningful experiences guiding the group of former Jesuits to the foundation and development of the Magister

Institute. This group was originally initiated by ten former Jesuits of Latin origin who after a period of distance and separation from the Society decided to approach the Jesuits and make a formal proposal to become their associates and collaborators. The chapter summarizes the qualitative method followed, heuristic-phenomenology, and the main parts of the study closely described and analyzed: the lived experiences of the founding group, the leadership strategies used to guide them through the creation and development of the Magister Institute, and the theological-philosophical paradigm of the Magister Institute as a part of the Christian Life Community. The study is a phenomenological-heuristic investigation based on the depictions made by the sample of the founding members and their closest collaborators and associates during this period of creation and development of the Magister Institute. The researcher is also a founding member of the Magister Institute. This requires an open and sincere scientific disposition on the part of the researcher to overcome possible limitations. In the chapter due consideration and critical analysis is given to the fact that the researcher is also a participant observer of the creation and development of the Magister Institute and that this situation may enhance the unity, clarity, and trustworthiness of the study.

CHAPTER II

REVIEW OF THE LITERATURE

Introduction

This chapter will review published literature relevant to the main ideas of this research study. The leadership strategies of the Executive Committee of the Magister Institute are connected to the psychological, educational, and pedagogical ideas of Carl Rogers (1961, 1969, 1977) and Paulo Freire (1969, 1970), and to their distinctive philosophical conception of person-centeredness and non-directiveness (Magister Institute collected papers, 2004-2009). Carl Rogers and Paulo Freire are not widely known for work in the areas of leadership and religious communities, yet, their influence in the creation and development of this concrete group was extraordinary (Magister Institute, members' reflections). Together with the ideas of Rogers and Freire, this chapter will review those of Lowney (2003) and Goleman (1995, 2002). This chapter will review their studies placing this proposal in the context of their contributions to Jesuit leadership research studies and to current conceptions of transformational leadership literature. Finally, this chapter will bring pertinent literature, though extracted from non-published sources, linking the philosophy and theoretical viewpoints of the members of Magister with the main theoretical expositions of the Christian Life Communities and the influential theological interpretations of Roberto Goizueta's critical writings (1995).

This chapter will discuss the following topics: Roger's-Freire Leadership Style, Non-Directiveness: Introduction, Basic Concepts: General, Historical review, Concept of Education, Socio-Political Context, Basic Concepts: Discussion, Discussion of Education, Socio-Political Context: Freire's Education for Liberation, Goleman's Leadership Studies, A New Rogers-Freire-Goleman Paradigm, Lowney's Jesuit Corporate Leadership Style, the Magister Institute and the Ex-Jesuits, the Christian Life Community and Goizueta's Challenge.

Rogers-Freire Leadership Style

The leadership approach followed by the Executive Committee of the group was important for the credibility and trustworthiness of the investigation. An insightful question for consideration was: Did this style of leadership an obstacle to the development of the group, or was it rather a catalyst of the group's development and ultimate accomplishment? This approach combines the nondirectiveness of Rogers' (1961, 1969, 1977) recommended interventions and the social conscientization strategies of the nonviolent method of Paulo Freire (1969). Freire's approach adds a much needed social and political awareness to Rogers' nondirectiveness and the necessary wisdom to make gains in the process of growth and commitment, which is a personal, religious, and social phenomenon. Actually, Rogers and Freire, when analyzed from the point of view of qualitative research paradigms, could be best inscribed in the phenomenological, heuristic, and ethnographic traditions of inquiry (Moustakas, 1990, 1994). Rogers's methodology uses the operational definitions of terms to make them objective and measurable, thus placing him half way between the experimental and qualitative nationwide traditions of doing research. Freire's theory of cultural action and conscientization falls close to the heuristic or within the critical ethnography paradigms. This former Jesuit group will have to cope with the issues of social justice and personal commitment; they will

MAGISTER: THE PHENOMENON OF MISSION AND
CAMARADERIE ROGERS-FREIRE FOR SOCIAL JUSTICE.

47

even have to face the issue of siding with the poor and underprivileged of this world (Magister Institute collected papers, 2004-2009). There is much of critical thinking (Freire, 1970) to be done during the process to which this group has committed itself.

Non-Directiveness: Introduction

The person-centered approach of today was known for many years as the client-centered style of counseling and psychotherapy, and was originally called nondirective counseling and psychotherapy (Rogers, 1942, 1951). The term indicated a new emphasis on the counseling/ therapeutic interview and is in clear contrast and opposition to the traditional dependence-creating relationship of psychoanalysis. For Carl Rogers (1961), the patient/client was the center and the owner of the process of therapy and cure, and had to be the one making the decisions and actually gaining the insight and being blessed with the enlightenment. The concept also provided a new kind of therapeutic activity: the psychotherapist should provide the necessary elements for an ideal therapeutic atmosphere to facilitate and promote the process of self-directiveness by the client.

The person-centered approach also implied both a philosophical concept and a concrete proposal for development and full realization of human nature (Rogers & Kinget, 1967). This new concept of therapy and human growth promoted certain personality traits more than others, and has envisioned a peculiar ideal of the fully functioning person (Hall, Lindzey, & Campbell, 1998). From these concepts, Rogers has presented a challenge to those leaders interested in the design and engineering of organizations, communities, and society (Rogers 1977; Solomon 1987; Swenson 1987).

Rogers has been criticized from two different angles. On one hand, B. F. Skinner thought that Rogers' concepts and methodology should not be considered a part of the true science of psychology. This confrontation had a climactic moment in the famous Rogers-Skinner dialogue or debate (Rogers & Skinner, 1956). The nondirective approach created a new movement in psychology known as the third force; the first being psychoanalysis and the second behaviorism (Hall et al., 1998). On the other hand, Rogers has found admirers and critics from the socioeconomic dimension of his theories and concepts. This present analysis will focus on the criticism coming from the eminent educator Paulo Freire. It is interesting to note that Rogers never met Freire, but he knew of Freire's work and methods of educational political activism in other countries. Rogers dedicated one chapter of his book "Carl Rogers on Personal Power" to Freire's concepts of oppression and liberation (Rogers, 1977).

Roger's ideas and concepts have been central to the movement known today as humanistic psychology, which was made up of existential psychologists and psychiatrists, encounter group theorists and practitioners, and many others who found the remaining two movements too constricting or asphyxiating (Hall et al., 1998). Rogers' ideas, concepts, and theories will be critically reviewed to integrate the following concepts into a new paradigm: freedom, teamwork, scientific discipline, social conscience, use of power, technology, and knowledge.

Basic Concepts: General Ideas

Rogers has always believed the human being capable of creative development from within since each person has intrinsically a positive direction (Cruz, 1983; Rogers & Knight, 1967). If Rogers postulated the necessity of a favorable atmosphere, he had in mind this interior creative potential for growth. He postulated a natural tendency in each one to realize or actualize self potential. This process derives from the actualization of the self. These tendencies should move the individual development in the direction of maturity and self-fulfillment if the requisites for growth and development are present. These requisites are unconditional positive regard, permissiveness, or lack of threats and judgments about the person, perception, and acceptance of this unconditional positive regard towards oneself by the clients (Rychlak, 1981). Rogers has insisted that, for growth to occur, it would take at least two interacting persons—one in congruence and another in a state of incongruence. This means that one of the two should be in touch with his or her interior world of experience with ease and accuracy, and thus help the other to accept himself or herself through a carefully designed psychological contact. This contact is the key since it could unleash a process of imitation and transference with the congruent person as its final cause. By definition, the congruent person has been found to be free, acceptant of self, in touch with his or her reality, and views this reality friendly (Rogers & Kinget, 1967). The fully functioning person has been described as the one open to his or her reality, who lives existentially and who exhibits a basic trust towards his or her organism (Rogers, 1961).

This was an attempt to describe the necessary conditions for the client's growth and development. Rogers who postulated the effectiveness of these therapeutic conditions must have believed that human nature was basically positive with an innate tendency towards actualization and integration (Hall et al., 1998). When nondirectiveness was stated, the emphasis was on empathic listening and not asking questions, reflection of feelings and not making judgments about the actions of the client, emphasis put on paraphrasing and summarizing the main ideas of the conversation and not on responding with new information and stories, and emphasis always on being a companion to the person's review of his or her life and not in engaging in discussions or debates of informative dialogues. Nondirectiveness has provided freedom, acceptance, permissiveness, empathic understanding, and absence of threats; it has confirmed that the other person is actually reciprocating this acceptance and this understanding at all times (Rylack, 1981).

When the term client-centered is invoked, the emphasis is on a therapeutic relationship with patients who pay for the visit and who are expected to be in charge of their own cure and who are therefore called clients. Rogerian therapy is respectful, treating all human beings as equal to one another, and Rogers leaves the direction of the process to the client. The professional has a role to play: to provide the atmosphere of unconditional positive regard and permissiveness, empathic understanding, and congruence. The emphasis is on a genuine relationship more than a nondirective technique coldly applied at a distance from the client. This authenticity in the relationship has driven a contemporary therapist to propose the concept of fallibility to take precedence over the nondirective technique (Kahn, 1999).

Today, the term person-centered is preferred over client-centered and nondirective, because it is shown to denote more respect for the individual in the relationship, and because it is more inclusive. This term and the idea of respect for the individual has spread to other branches of knowledge such as counseling, education, group processes, international conflicts, political action, and leadership styles (Barrett-Lennard, 1994; Brink, 1987).

Nondirective and person-centered concepts have been integrated into a theory of development and growth, interpersonal relations, group processes, organizational management and leadership, education, counseling, and psychotherapy. Rogers has shown a unique understanding of human behavior and has prided himself in developing his concepts from research and in testing his hypotheses on objective scientific grounds. Rogers was a practitioner and an academic professor dedicated to objective research (Ewen, 1998; Hall & Lindzey, 1978; Hall et al., 1998). What was the Rogerian philosophy of science (Slife & Williams, 1995)? Rogers wanted to study the behavior of clients and whatever was related to their life. His main scientific tool was the operational definition, which he used to bridge the gap between concepts, ideas, theories, objective research, scientific method, and science (Moustakas, 1990, 1994). Rogers thought that the scientific method must be adapted to study human behavior and not vice versa. He understood the difficulty of making objective sense of the most subjective of realities. When B. F. Skinner (1956) criticized him for not studying human behavior on a small scale and for not sticking to only directly observable behaviors, he responded by rejecting Skinner's definition of science stemming from a safely and strategically chosen narrow concept of the scientific method. Rogers believed in objective rules of research but has become famous for defining in operational terms abstract concepts such as self, unconditional positive regard, and congruence, making them vulnerable to scientific empirical research

MAGISTER: THE PHENOMENON OF MISSION AND
CAMARADERIE ROGERS-FREIRE FOR SOCIAL JUSTICE.

51

(Ewen, 1998; Hall et al., 1998; Moustakas, 1990, 1994; Rychlak 1981).
Rogers was the first to allow the recording and videotaping of therapy
sessions for scientific methodological reasons (Hall et al.). Rogers
criticized behaviorists for their voluntary subjection to an outdated
logical positivistic philosophy of physical science in detriment of a
better understanding of behaviors, exclusively characteristic of human
beings (Rogers, 1985; Slife & Williams, 1995; Zucker, 1996). Rogers
confronted Skinner for a deterministic concept of behavior and human
beings (Rogers & Skinner, 1956). His nondirective school preferred the
phenomenological and heuristic method, but always adhered to a rigid
research protocol (Moustakas, 1990, 1994). Rogers has been considered
a moderate scientific rationalist (Slife & Williams, 1995) who studied
objectively the behaviors, thoughts, and feelings of free human beings
in their struggle for integration, growth, and existential functioning
as individuals and as members of communities and nations (Berett-
Lennard, 1994; Brink, 1987; Kahn, 1999; O'Hara, 1985; Quinn, 1993;
Rychlak, 1981; Solomon, 1987; Swenson, 1987).

Historical Review

In his early studies, Rogers (1942, 1951) developed the techniques
and the fundamentals, which made up the code of discipline and the
main strategies of his approach to therapy. As Rychlak (1981), Rogers
and Kinget (1967), and Hall et al. (1998) have pointed out, Rogers, in
his first decade, worked on the necessary and sufficient conditions to
guarantee empathic understanding and absence of threats to the client.
Freedom and respect, nondirectiveness, and client-centeredness were the
clear focal points for the creation of the Rogerian paradigm.

In 1963, his book *On Becoming a Person* went a step further in the
direction of a process concept of therapy, growth, and development.
The fully functioning person with peaceful and dynamic trust in the
organism became the highlight of the new Rogerian era. Encounter
groups (Ewen, 1998; Hall et al., 1998; Rogers, 1970; Swenson, 1987)
for persons in search of personal growth and a more fluid experience of

life became the main attraction of the movement in the United States and Europe.

Concept of Education

With his book *Freedom to Learn*, Rogers (1969) opened up his system to include teaching and learning in institutions. His movement extended its reach beyond counseling and psychotherapy into general education and was called the person-centered approach. According to Ewen (1998), Rogers considered the educational system to be widely influenced by a coercive and authoritarian philosophy. Highly directive and power-hungry teachers reinforced students' passivity and submissive attitudes. Exams and tests promoted parrot-like behaviors of learning. He found generalized lack of trust in teachers' constant monitoring of student progress. He denounced the recourse to tricky questions and unfair grading styles as widespread practices among teachers everywhere. He highlighted the total prominence placed on thinking skills with the consequent obliteration of the emotional dimension of experience portrayed as meaningless and not scholarly (Rogers, 1969; Goleman, 1995). The best students gave up on education and learning because they did not find it pleasant, meaningful, or relevant enough. Rogers (1977) said that school systems were "primarily institutions for incarcerating or taking care of the young, to keep them out of the adult world" (p. 256). He described the basic elements of nondirective teaching: the creation of a permissive climate, which fostered the students' capacity to think and learn for themselves. Rogers believed that empathy, unconditional positive regard, and transparency (congruence) were the key processes that would bring out the potential for learning present in every student. Rogerian methodology implied shared decision making by a group of students. Students in a group were responsible for their own program of learning. The teacher's role is to act as a resource person or coordinator. There are no class presentations and no structure to follow. Each group needed to meet with the facilitator and develop a plan based on earlier performance

and mutually accepted assessment procedures and to be able to teach
from the syllabus in order to meet the preestablished grade at the end
of the semester. Work completed included evidence of the amount of
personal and educational growth achieved by each student during the
length of the course. Rogers believed that this self-directed teaching
style provided the individual with new possibilities to enjoy the process
of education where the climate of permissiveness and nonstructured
and empathic teaching fostered creativity in the direction that could be
most rewarding to each student. In the Rogerian learning methodology,
the new students are thrown into a group and the group is made
responsible for choosing and designing the content of the syllabus, the
desired procedures for evaluation, and scheduling the meetings and
arranging the format of the meetings to discuss the material selected.
But this approach to teaching could also arouse a state of uncertainty
for those students who are accustomed to a structured and organized
form of learning as coming from an authoritative figure in the academic
world (Rogers, 1969, 1977).

Socio-Political Context: Rogers
on Personal Power

Carl Rogers (1977) signaled the end of a process of reflection of the
person-centered approach. He and his followers were concerned with
the relation and usefulness of their thoughts and theories to the so-
called oppressed people. Not used to such terminology, Rogers followed
Paulo Freire's (1970) *Pedagogy of the Oppressed.* Freire was a famous
Latin American educator, born in Brazil, who taught at Harvard for
many years and the Executive Board of Harvard Educational Review
considered him an educator who influenced and touched the entire
world (Brizuela & Soler-Gallart, 1998).

Rogers (1977) thought that politics was the process of obtaining,
using, sharing or abandoning power, control, and participation in the
decision-making process. Rogers saw the human being as a powerful
person, and he maintained this approach in education. He believed that

education did not give power to anybody, but neither was education supposed to take this power away from the person in the first place. The person-centered educators/facilitators insist that this approach is based on the concept of liberating the human being as man should be considered a trustworthy organism. These liberators view the human being as capable of self-understanding and self-determination (Bakan, 1996). However, Rogers thought that the educational, industrial, and military systems in the United States had an intrinsically radically contrasting view that, "the nature of the individual is such that you cannot trust in him/her; that he/she must be guided, instructed, rewarded, punished, and controlled by those who are wiser, or belong to a superior status" (Rogers, 1977, p. 5).

Rogers (1977) believed that with a proper psychological climate this internal inclination of the individual (personal power) can be released. Rogers believed that this growth-promoting climate has three basic characteristics: authenticity or congruence, unconditional positive regard, and empathic understanding. If the aforementioned conditions were present in a relationship between facilitator and oppressed, student and teacher, counselor and client, the following would result:

> From a political standpoint, by accepting his/her inner feelings, the client reduces the power others have had over him/her to inculcate guilt, fear and inhibitions upon him/her. Little by little his acceptance and control over himself increases. The more he/she accepts him/herself the bigger and bigger he/she becomes. The client possesses him/herself in a way he/she has never before. The feeling of power is growing. The more the client accepts him/herself, the more he/she is conscious of him/herself, the less defensive and more open he becomes finding at last some of the necessary freedom to grow and to change in the natural direction of the human organism. Now life is in his/her hands to be lived like an individual. (Rogers, 1977, p. 7)

As a conclusion, Rogers mentioned five conditions which, if met, would guarantee a liberation process, which was supported also by Freire. Rogers described this joint liberation proposal in 12 points.

Basic Concepts: Discussion

There were a few general criticisms to the nondirective, client-centered, and/or person-centered theory of Carl Rogers. Attention was called to its naïve conception of human nature and society as a whole, to the methodology of research as being too qualitative and the main concepts of its theory being too general and embracing, to the lack of dialogue and information giving taking place in the interview, to its definition of self-concept in relation only to conscious experience, to the little value the nondirective theorists had afforded to unconscious behavior and its impact in personality development, and finally, attention was called to the nondirective nature of the therapeutic relationship and the possibility of introducing the concept of fallibility as a better means of understanding the deeper nature of person-centeredness (Barrett-Lennard, 1994; Brink, 1987; Ewen, 1998; Hall et al., 1998; Kahn, 1999; O'Hara, 1985; Quinn, 1993; Rychlak, 1981; Solomon, 1987; Swenson, 1987).

No doubt this person-centered school of psychology has developed a well thought out theory of human behavior. The firm basis on empirical research has made the person-centered approach gain respect in academic and professional circles with the capacity to generate research. This according to the classic authors, Hall, Lindzey, and Campbell, of *Theories of Personality* was the most important characteristic of a psychological system or theory of personality (Hall et al., 1998). Rogerian theorists and counselors proclaimed that it was important for all to be treated as equal, respected for what they are, and be given a chance to prove what they are from within if given the opportunity (Rogers & Kinget, 1967). These concepts and theories they tested had the same results when applied to the practice of counseling and psychotherapy, education, marriage, community living, and peaceful negotiations among nations and groups (Barrett, 1994; Solomon, 1987; Swenson, 1987).

The concept of nondirectiveness was a target of criticism (Kahn, 1999; Quinn, 1993). Basically, nondirective techniques involved reflection of feelings, paraphrasing, and summarizing as vehicles to arrive at empathic understanding. Unconditional positive regard and the required congruence or transparency on the part of the counselor together with empathic understanding would provide the necessary conditions (psychological climate) for therapy to be successful. The reality of therapy was that the counselor often made no comments, added no information, confronted no statement, did not alert to past or possible alternative behavior or consequence because the nondirective counselor wanted the clients to receive no influence from the therapist and be left to themselves for the direction the process would or could have taken. This left clients rather on their own, often lacking the necessary information or the awakening call to move forward and make the required change. As Kahn (1999) so brilliantly explained, if all therapists would agree that there is always healthy information to be provided, there are times when this information is more needed, such as in therapy. Then why not have the counselor give it to the client? The answer could have hinted at the necessity of protecting the client from undue external influence and to the simultaneous requirement of the approach to keep direction at all times in the hands of the client and out of the hands of the therapist. This could be done, first by providing the same kind of climate Rogers had so carefully delineated, and second, by making the client experience the fallibility of the counselor's comments and opinions. This could guarantee that the clients/students would have to actively weigh the information provided to them by their counselors or facilitators and make a decision whether to follow it or not. This fallible attitude must be cultivated through a process of checks and balances: treating the clients/students as equal, allowing the clients/students to disagree or think differently, and provoking instances where the clients/students would necessarily arrive at a different opinion.

Discussion of Education

The basic ideas of the person-centered approach to education were perceived as clear and as a radical application of the therapeutic principles themselves (Rogers, 1969, 1977). If the concept of fallibility were accepted, a whole new dimension would be added for information giving, dialogue, confrontation, and even debate. This would have made the teacher a more active and human facilitator capable of valuable input and feedback (Kahn, 1999).

The experience of shared responsibility for learning, at least between the student and the facilitator, has been noteworthy. Nevertheless, the criticism that Rogerian educational theory is basically individualistic still has remained unanswered. It has certainly provided the individual with a more rewarding personal experience but ultimately, there is no give-and-take characteristic of real-life situations of group participation. Two elements could have been added to this group to make it closer to a "shared experience" in real life: To have made the syllabus a group project and to have enforced the final grade as the average of the individual grades of the members of the group. This would create a very tense situation for those used to getting good grades in prior assignments and then facing the possibility of having to share the grade with less fortunate or less effort-guided individuals. It would have made the participation in the group closer to the real world and made one's grade dependent on somebody else's decision to study hard and actually learn. Any kind of learning or achievement would have to be critically evaluated as part of the new way of teaching.

This experience of full submersion into a social learning situation cannot and should not be extended to all subjects, but with the student's consent could be allowed for a two-semester course in a determined subject. This could then be a very promising training experience for a group of boys or girls who play basketball, soccer, or football together in a team. In the games, as in real life, the winning score is the sum of the efforts and achievements of each one (Rogers, 1969).

Socio-Political Context: Freire's
Education for Liberation

Rogers did not mention any great difference between Paulo Freire's (1970) Pedagogy of the Oppressed and his person-centered approach to education (Rogers, 1977). For Freire, however, the oppressed must create a psychosocial climate of dialogue with the help of the facilitator in the midst of his own oppressive existential socioeconomic situation, and with the aid of a new critical method of analysis.

This submersion into dialogue, as described by Freire (1969, 1970), had a twofold aim: to make a diagnosis of the existential situation of the oppressed and to facilitate their encounter with each other in the middle of their dramatic reality. There was dialectics involved here between the oppressed and their existential socioeconomic situation. For Freire, the oppressed had to change their conscience into a transformational one which was not innate to them and which would not develop and grow except under certain specific conditions where they throw themselves into a debate, with a critical examination of their problems and those of their group and community. In this debate, the oppressed would have to take an active part. For liberation to have any chance, the oppressed have to change their frame of mind. There is a need for education for decision making as well as for political and social responsibility. This point is crucial in Freire's education for liberation pedagogy and it is found to be at odds with Rogers' central notion. Education cannot make any miracles in the midst of a changeless society. If there are no changes in society there can be no possibility for an education for liberation. The value of education for Freire was considered instrumental and "it will be null if it were superimposed to the conditions of the social context where it is to be applied" (Freire, 1969, p. 7). So for Freire, the value and effectiveness of education is considered to be a function of the dynamics for change present in the socio-cultural environment. Reality, as it is and not as it is conceived by the oppressed, was what mattered in Freire's Pedagogy. Liberation was understood as a dialectical effort of an education imaged in social and political responsibility. This was basically the joint effort of both the method and the necessary facilitating climate. The facilitator has a great deal to do with the application of the method and the creation of the climate. Education for liberation always implies a critical attitude; the oppressed have to understand their situation in their context. There has to be active participation, integration, and objective representation of reality. Conscientization thus becomes the development of this new critical attitude; social and economic transformations cannot affect these changes in the frame of mind of the oppressed if there is no critical education. There must be a critical pedagogic work based on favorable historic situations. There must be a substitution of a magic interpretation of social and economic affairs for new critical causal explanations.

Rogers considered it of utmost importance and usefulness to understand the world of the client oppressed from the client's internal frame of reference. For Freire, more important than this phenomenological personal world has been the objective socioeconomic reality out there. The oppressed client has to understand it objectively and critically. Rogers put no emphasis in the methodology required for the client or oppressed individual to comprehend the socioeconomic reality out there as it really is and he shows no interest in helping clients understand their own reality as it really is. Rogers presupposed that the absence of threats and the presence of psychological climate, full with unconditional positive regard and empathic understanding, were sufficient for personal growth to take place automatically in the direction of self-management and self-understanding. The two approaches were found to be different and sometimes even in clear opposition to each other.

Goleman's Leadership Studies

The Jesuits were founded in 1534 by Ignatius of Loyola from Spain (Iparraguirre, 1963). Since then, they have become one of the leading male religious organizations to integrate the Catholic Church (Drucker, 1999; Lowney, 2003; Roberts, 1993). As late as 1980, a leader of the Italian government publicly declared that the Jesuits formed the model of the Italian political culture (McDonough, 1992). McDonough points out that the Jesuits integrate better than any other group, handling live tensions in Catholicism between modernity and tradition (McDonough). The Jesuits are central to this study because the ten original members of the Magister Institute who met to discuss the possibilities of doing some religious work together were former Jesuits, and five of them were also ordained Jesuit priests (Magister Institute collected papers, 2004). A major work by McDonough and Bianchi (2002) relates the Jesuit and ex-Jesuit experience in the last 30 years. The authors claim that, from just before the Vatican II Council of 1960 to the turn of the millennium, the Society of Jesus in the United States of America has declined from over 5,000 to less than 4,000 members. According to these authors, only in India has there been a slight increase in numbers, although lately there has been a slight decline similar to the one in the United States. In the Antilles Province, which includes Cuba, Dominican Republic, and Miami-Dade County of Florida, the numbers have also declined, though the number of Cubans and Dominicans leaving quite exceeds those joining and staying (J. Saez, personal communication, December 2008). Of the six young adults who entered the novitiate in 1959 in El Calvario, Havana, Cuba, only two have remained (J. Saez, personal communication, December 2008). This study illustrates the reality of the talent, the positive attitudes, and the readiness of hundreds and thousands of former Jesuits who could join other Jesuits and religious in daily and specialized apostolic activities. This study, via interviews and other collected materials, will bring out the feelings involved in the process of re-acceptance and re-association. According to McDonough and Bianchi (2002), the older Jesuits, whose unity and camaraderie were that of a military sort of loyalty, used to consider those leaving the Order as traitors and unworthy of their trust. In the last decade, nevertheless, changes have been steadily occurring, and those leaving are treated with compassion, permitting communication between those leaving and those continuing in the religious organization.

Since this chapter is concerned with leadership styles of the Jesuits in general and of this group of former Jesuits in particular, it is justifiable to examine the historical elements linking scholars in the areas of transformational leadership, the type of management style of the Jesuits, and the leadership style of the Executive Committee members of the Magister Institute. Goleman (1995), the author chosen by former Jesuit Chris Lowney (2003) as one of the most salient scholars in today's global leadership movement, confirms the overall effectiveness and uniqueness of the 450-year old heroic style of Jesuit leadership. Goleman belongs to the transformational leadership school of thought (Henderson & Hawthorne, 2000; Hickman, 1998). Goleman has published several books and has become a pioneer in a new direction in transformational leadership studies (Goleman, Boyatzis, & McKee, 2002). Goleman provides research in the central issue of emotional intelligence and has synthesized his results in a few interrelated concepts as adapted by Lowney. The main attribute of Goleman's concept of emotional intelligence is self-awareness and relates to the capacity to understand one's feelings, changes of mood, and stable temperament (O'Neil, 1996).

The second dimension of the concept of emotional intelligence has to do with the ability of the subject to integrate and control or at least redirect negative impulses and mood changes. This ability is mostly self-regulatory. The third dimension is related to whatever produces impetus for leadership. Usually concepts such as vision, mission, and goals are closely related with motivation to work with passion for reasons transcending money and status. The fourth dimension of emotional intelligence, empathy, is the central concept of the Rogerian and the Jesuit leadership styles. Goleman (1995) looks at empathy as the ability to understand the other person from an emotional point of view.

Finally, Goleman (1995), from a different angle, considers the ability to manage relationships and build networks, focus on the capacity to negotiate common ground, and build an emotional and friendly relationship with others. Goleman considers this ability to become proficient in social skills as essential to the building of a relationship based on mutual trust and feelings, and a deep common understanding.

A New Rogers-Freire-Goleman Paradigm

This literature review and analysis has laid the foundations for a review of the transformational theories of leadership in a critical way. This critical review provides a discussion of the findings and conclusions of the transformational leadership current literature, as represented by one of its primary proponents. Since these authors represent a good sample of the published literature relevant to the main topic of this study, this analysis will help clarify the conception of leadership of the Executive Committee of the Magister Institute.

Daniel Goleman's Emotional Intelligence (1995) has developed a provocative profile of the 21st century leader. Goleman has postulated five domains of emotional intelligence: self-awareness, self-regulation, motivation, empathy, and social skills. According to Goleman, these factors of emotional intelligence have been found to have more relevance in successful management than any other including classical IQ scores.

The first domain of emotional intelligence, self-awareness, was understood as the ability to know one's emotions (Goleman, 1995, 2002). Individuals have attained a level of mastery of this domain when they recognize feelings and emotions as they occur. In the nondirective person-centered approach, this concept is similar to congruence and transparency, which are absolutely necessary for therapy to take place at any level, for education to be facilitated, for liberation to be effective in any place. Rogers looks at congruence as a measure of freedom from inner tension that gives oneself a reading of psychological adjustment achieved up to that moment. "When self-experiences are accurately symbolized, and are included in the self-concept in this accurately symbolized form, then the state is one of congruence of self and experience" (Rychlak, 1981, p. 589). Rogers (1977) goes a step further in that he requires the counselor to be feeling that way and to be able to show it to the client(s). Congruence meant freedom for Rogers—a person in harmony and at peace. This kind of human being can be fully capable of handling the task at hand and can be imitated without developing dependency (a transference which takes the freedom away

MAGISTER: THE PHENOMENON OF MISSION AND
CAMARADERIE ROGERS-FREIRE FOR SOCIAL JUSTICE.

63

from the other). These two concepts are one and the same, and the importance given to it by Goleman, Rogers, and Freire is also striking: *a conditio sine qua non.*

Self-regulation of emotional behaviors, the second domain of emotional intelligence, could be contrasted with self-directedness and self-determination, goals of Rogerian educational practices, group process experiences, and personal growth and development. According to Bakan (1996), it is also the goal of psychology and the goal of the day-to-day struggle of the oppressed in dialectical confrontation with their surroundings and in psychological empathic contact with the facilitator (Freire, 1970). How one handles feelings is the measure of growth and achievement in the direction of self-determination. What matters about the comparison is that Rogers and Freire have described and been through many experiences as facilitators, the process by which self-regulation can be attained. Briefly, a person in need looks for the help of another in state of congruence, capable of showing transparency, who can provide to the interested client unconditional positive regard and who can elicit from the client positive responses making it evident through them that empathic understanding is being continually achieved. If this process occurs, Rogers and Freire guarantee that self-direction, self-regulation, and self-determination are being achieved (Rogers, 1961, 1977; Freire, 1970). This concept should make trainers of managers or CEOs understand the importance of selecting appropriate mentors to guide high caliber individuals through the training and development processes (Gouillart & Kelly, 1995). These mentors must be trained.

Empathy is a third key concept of emotional intelligence, and for Rogers and Freire it is the necessary companion to the other two. Rogers looks at empathy as the byproduct of unconditional positive regard and expects from the leader or counselor an attitude of congruence/transparency. According to Rogers (1961, 1977) and Freire (1970) there is no way one can attain self-direction or self-regulation without a psychological climate of which empathic understanding is a key third ingredient. Both Rogers and Freire consider the basic role of the facilitator is to help the client attain self-understanding. Therefore, the counselor/

facilitator tries to summarize and paraphrase in intellectual and clear language what the client has said in an obscure and emotional way. This effort will not be successful until the counselor/facilitator reflects not only the meanings but especially the feelings that accompany those meanings. To be understood is a great feeling, but to be empathically understood is a growth-stimulating experience. CEOs, and trainers and developers of personnel should realize the importance of this specific skill for those interested in leadership positions. This is the key and fundamental people skill. Empathy can be acquired, and can be improved upon. CEOs should bear in mind that empathy can only be taught by congruent/transparent facilitators; those who can afford to provide unconditional positive regard. It is difficult to genuinely and sincerely make unconditional positive regard a part of one's daily effort to communicate and understand other people. Here, the importance of the fallibility concept should be mentioned as explained by Kahn (1999). Once empathic understanding takes place and is mutually perceived, and once the clients feel that they are unconditionally accepted for what they are, then an atmosphere of mutual respect and understanding has been formed. This is the time for the counselors to work on the fallibility concept. The counselors should not allow the clients to accept their words and opinions as infallible, impossible to be flawed, or erroneous. The proper atmosphere of equal respect and fallibility will pave the way for a true dialogue and enriching communication of vital information.

In their organizational vision, leaders often do not include the real growth and genuine development of the members of their organization. When they do, these concepts are particularly relevant since they are based on research and professional clinical experience (Rogers, 1977).

Motivation, as the energy necessary to take any assignment and follow it through successfully, is a byproduct of a fully functioning person who is open to experience, lives existentially (in a fluid way, in basically a congruent continual state), and is capable of establishing empathic relations with other human beings (Rogers, 1963, 1977). When empathy is absent from one's life, and when there are no signs of relationships of unconditional positive regard, then there should be reason to believe that the motivational level of the person will be low.

Viktor Frankl (1996) maintains that motivation is a function of goals and purposes that are valued by a person. For his logotherapeutic concept of motivation, one needs goals and purposes for the motivation level to rise automatically. Frankl believes that if one has reason to live (a loved one, a book to write, a career to pursue), one will have the motivation to survive almost anything. For Frankl, if life is conceptualized as a mission in response to somebody or something stimulating, there will always be meaning and motivation. This concept of motivation should be closely related to the general vision of the organization and to the mission statement, which summarizes the vision of the organization and makes it appealing and attractive to its members. The role of the leader is key in providing the necessary atmosphere, vision, and mission statement to capture each member's heart and mind every single day.

The last domain of the emotional intelligence concept is social skills or team building (Goleman, 1995, 2002). It is difficult to attain this skill because it presupposes a healthy personality at peace with oneself, in control of one's emotions and feelings, capable of unconditional positive regard and empathic understanding, and genuinely interested in contacting, helping, guiding, and encouraging others in the direction of development and growth, both personal and institutional. This concept implies a rather fulfilled human being, committed with the vision of the organization and with the journey of each of its members. This person must possess vision, ideals, congruence, and authentic interest for the growth and development of others.

Finally, it is important to make a statement about self-directed teams in management. Kimball Fisher's (1993) Self-Directed Work Teams are a group of employees who are given responsibility to manage themselves with minimum direct supervision. These teams belong to a level of the most advanced form of empowerment. They are committed to the work ethic and to their customers more than to their managers. They are a new form of self-determined, self-directed, self-regulated individuals working in a tight knit group performing multilevel tasks in an organization. They are trained to be responsible and to act independently. Their approach is a byproduct of long analysis when applied to a business organization. People have a natural inclination to succeed (Freire, 1969, 1970; Rogers, 1951, 1963, 1967, 1977) or can be trained to be self-regulated and self-directed (Fisher, 1993).

Lowney's Jesuit Corporate Leadership Style

A specific dimension of Jesuit life is their leadership style that is described briefly following the main ideas of former Jesuit Chris Lowney (2003). Jesuit leadership strategies are part of the implicit basis of the Magister Institute's leadership repertoire. According to Lowney (2003), since the time of Ignatius of Loyola, the Jesuits have developed and honed a style of leadership based on four strategies. These governing principles and interpersonal philosophy were part of the essence of the Jesuit way of life and Ignatian spirituality and were expected of each one of the Jesuits in their relations with the world at large, and were also to be used for the education and management of the Jesuits themselves. Self-awareness, ingenuity, love, and heroism are the four charged words best describing this Jesuit leadership managerial style. The Jesuits are trained continuously to know and understand themselves, to check on their weaknesses and strengths in their daily meditative practices, and, again, more intensively during special prolonged introspective time periods yearly. The Jesuits also undergo a deep self evaluation twice in their lifetimes (Lowney, 2003).

The Jesuits have a good grasp of themselves, their value system, and world view. Chosen and trained to become innovators, self-confident amidst change, and looking ahead in the direction of a new and better world, they are encouraged continually in their training to make their own decisions and come up with new and challenging ideas (Drucker, 1999; Roberts, 1993). Conformity, according to Lowney (2003), is not a part of the Jesuit educational manual. With self-knowledge and creative adapting to the future, the Jesuits teach their own to relate genuinely and affectionately to others, especially to one another. The Jesuit *esprit-de-coeur*, camaraderie, and love for one another is proverbial (Lowney). Heroism, the last of the leadership strategies of the Jesuit training manual, is characterized by wholeheartedly following Christ, the great king and leader, in one key passage of the Ignatian Spiritual Exercises. This total commitment to a cause in an intense and continuous manner is what constitutes the heroic Jesuit leadership, always demanding *magis* or more of themselves, and always spreading their wings to embrace more and more, since Ignatius of Loyola put no limits to the intensity of commitment, the spread of the love and the apostolic zeal of each Jesuit (Iparraguirre, 1963; Lowney, 2003; McDonough & Bianchi, 2002).

These strategies are part of the Jesuit tradition and usually manifest themselves in their corporate works. The segment of this chapter, on the group of former Jesuits that met each other and proceeded to find common grounds until the Magister Institute was finally formed, will be described in a preparatory manner with information and materials found in the Magister Institute collected papers. These first general descriptions are open to receive like final forms the definitive phenomenological depictions provided by the definitive series of interviews of the main research.

The Magister Institute and the Former Jesuits

The Magister Institute is made up of ten male former Jesuits, extremely well educated and with a personal history of pastoral, educational, political, and religious leadership. These former Jesuits separated and kept a distance from the Jesuit Order (Magister Institute collected papers, 2004). All of these former Jesuits had spent two to 20 years as Jesuits in training. Only one had completed the entire training and had taken the final vows. It was evident early on that the entire group had retained their admiration for the Jesuits, but several members indicated that there was little hope of being of any interest to the Jesuits, both in Miami and in the Dominican Republic (Antilles Province). Most of them, however, retained a strong desire to reconnect with their religious and ethnic roots (Magister Institute collected papers, 2004). Since many of these individuals felt strongly against initiating or resuming any contact with the Jesuits, it was very difficult to start any communication pointing in a new direction of re-association with the Jesuits. The kind of leadership style used from the first meeting provided guidance for the complexities of the feelings and emotions of the members of the group (Magister Institute collected papers, 2007). On the one hand, a Rogerian person-centered and nondirective approach was considered, and on the other hand, a critical pedagogic reading of the situations was also entertained based on the Freirian critical and nondirective leadership style. This dual approach helped to gather the group and open the doors to a new direction congruent with the group's philosophy and Jesuit training and education.

The Christian Life Community and Goizueta's Challenge

The former Jesuits developed an idea of apostolic community that was very similar to the one already institutionalized by the Society of Jesus as the continuation of the old sodalities or Marian congregations (Christian Life Community, Principios Generales de la Comunidad de Vida Cristiana, 1991; Magister Institute, Principios Generales del Instituto Magister, 2004). The former Jesuits emphasized discernment, prayer, preferential option for the poor, and produced a model of government very similar to the one of Comunidad de Vida Cristiana. They both had a coordinator, an Executive Committee, and were supposed to be intrinsically apostolic communities. They both believed in the spiritual exercises of Ignatius of Loyola as the brain and heart center of their spiritual, social, and personal lives. The way the Society of Jesus understands and extends the interpretation of the spiritual exercises is the norm for the group's understanding and interpretation. The association with the Jesuits was slowly transformed into a sort of accompaniment in the sense that Goizueta (1995) understood it. Goizueta is the only son of a very rich Cuban American who studied theology against his father's will and became the President of the Academy of Catholic Hispanic Theologians of the United States (1990-1991) and President of the Catholic Theological Society of America

(2004-2005). Today, Dr. Roberto Goizueta teaches systematic theology at Boston College, a well known Jesuit College (Magister Institute 2005 Goizueta, *Goizueta's DVD: la Virgen, los pobres y Magister*). The relation with the Jesuits slowly became one of mutual friendliness and respect. This fresh and open rapport came about as the byproduct of the personal charisma and gifted approaches of several Jesuits of the Miami Community and the Jesuit Provincial Superior of the Antilles Province (Magister Institute collected papers, 2004-2009; J. Zaglul, personal communication, December, 2004; P. Suarez, personal communication, December, 2004).

The Magister Institute community had several special features that demanded discussion, debate, and caused some turbulence. Miami is the center of the Cuban-American exile community, and consequently, the feelings and emotions are raw and exposed when social issues come under discussion (Goizueta, 1995; Portes & Bach, 1985; San Juan Cafferty & McCready, 1992). The discussions in the elaboration of the Magister's General Principles (Principios Generales) were civil and approved by consensus (Magister Institute collected papers, foundation meetings). Later on, when the membership was large and composed of men and women, the discussions about social issues and political participation were passionate and at times turned out to be uncivil (Magister Institute members' reflections, 2004-2009). The nondirective style of leadership, a natural phenomenon when the founding six former Jesuits were the only members was a dynamic and simultaneously a unifying cohesive force. When the group grew larger and each man's wife was integrated into the group, the non-directive leadership style was also a plus for this group to survive heated and sensitive discussions, and debate, without disruption (Magister Institute collected papers, 2004-2009; reflections, 2004-2009). The group coalesced and remained of one mind, at least formally, even though there were several conflictive, difficult, and unavoidable moments (Magister Institute collected papers, members' reflections, 2004-2009). For some, these moments of political and social disagreements culminated in the split of the group in two (Magister Institute members' reflections, 2004-2009).

The preferential option for the poor (i.e., to work for and defend their cause), which is a significant commitment required of all members by the General Principles of the Christian Life Communities, became a difficult issue to accept by some group members, and a very touchy subject interpreted in different ways by some other members (Magister Institute collected papers, members' reflections, 2004-2008). The members of the Executive Committee were challenged several times in their efforts to appease or promote order and mutual respect (Magister Institute collected papers, members' reflections, 2004-2008). When the proposition to have Our Lady of Guadalupe as Magister's Special Patroness was brought up; and when Goizueta's (2005) challenge to adopt an option to work with the Latinos in the United States and recognize them as inclusive and part of the group's commitment to the poor was formally introduced, the internal differences and disagreements were highlighted (Magister Institute, Goizueta's DVD: La Virgen, los pobres y Magister, 2005). This conceptual framework and the discussions about its interpretations were few, but very exhaustive (Magister Institute Collected Papers, Members' Reflections, 2004-2008). Following the nondirective approach of leadership, the Executive Committee divided the group into two for half the time of the weekly meetings, and assigned two new facilitators for the meetings. This strategy brought more peace and harmony to the group; although the issues were never definitely resolved (Magister Institute collected papers, members' reflections, 2004-2008). Goizueta's conception of the group's commitments was not accepted by some of the members. Therefore, resorting to the nondirective approach, the group continued in a kind of workable truce and reconciliation (Magister Institute collected papers, members' reflections, 2004-2008).

The nondirective character of Magister's leadership style and their deep level of spiritual commitment (Magister Institute collected papers, Members' Reflections, 2004-2008) were key factors in accepting the dissenting members into a new community, and both separate and friendly groups continued their quest as members of the same network of World and National Christian Communities (Magister Institute collected papers, members' reflections, 2004-2008).

Chapter Summary

This chapter presented a review of the literature related to the central issues of this research study. It introduced and discussed the literature necessary to understand the synthesis of leadership style of Rogers and Freire in their context. It reviewed the concepts of non-directiveness, and the general ideas necessary to comprehend the leadership strategies stemming from their common thoughts when applied to the creation and development of a small group or community. The literature pertinent to the understanding of the concepts of Freire and Rogers about education was also presented and reviewed. The socio-cultural and political context of Rogers, as found in the published literature, was also reviewed, mostly based on his book "on personal power." The discussion and critical analysis of non-directiveness, education, and socio-political context, as found in the published literature, was also examined. A critical review of the published literature basic to the understanding of emotional intelligence, empathic understanding, congruence and transparency was discussed in the context of Goleman's description of the 21th century leader, Lowney's Jesuit leadership style, and Rogerian-Freirian leadership guidelines, and was presented as a tentative sketch for a new paradigm. The chapter offered a connection of the former Jesuits with the current Jesuit leadership style as described by a former Jesuit Carl Lowney (2003). It made a description of the origins of the Magister Institute through the collected papers gathered by the group as part of its history. The chapter described and explained the theoretical and philosophical basis both of the Magister Institute (Goizueta, 1995) and of the leadership styles of the Executive Committee of the Magister Institute (Rogers, 1963, 1977; Freire, 1968, 1970). The descriptions of the Jesuit style of leadership, their philosophical and theoretical connections with Goleman's studies, and finally their congruence with the Rogerian/Freirian leadership and managerial styles were also analyzed and attempts were made to bring forth a theoretical synthesis. Finally, this chapter also discussed the relevance of the experiences these former Jesuits went through in the stages described: from separation to reunion, from reunion to possible re-association, and from there to the perceived present stage of collaboration. The chapter ends describing the current situation of both groups sharing common origin and philosophical kinship.

CHAPTER III
METHODOLOGY

Introduction

Chapter III describes the methodology and research design of this study. The chapter explains the reasons for selecting the framework upon which the research was based. This section also describes the population and sample selected, and includes an explanation of the research question that guided this study. The methods that were followed in the process of data collection and the strategies of analysis used by the researcher are also described and clarified. Finally, this chapter provides the strategies and methods used to guarantee the ethical nature and trustworthiness of the results of this study.

The documentation that was used as evidence for this study included the narratives of research participants and the researcher, and evidence collected in interviews, notes, artifacts, movies, videotapes, photographs, and any other relevant personal documents. All related documents were used to elucidate and enrich the narrative of each of the active participants, and were not used to interpret meanings that were not evident in the research participants' experiences (Moustakas, 1990, 1994). Only the dialogue between the research participants and the researcher served to clarify, enrich, and reinterpret their narratives. This section of enrichment and dialogue was guided by the work of

Clark Moustakas, a leading scholar and researcher in phenomenological studies (Creswell, 1998, 2005; Denzin & Lincoln, 1998), and in phenomenological heuristic research (Moustakas, 1990, 1994).

This phenomenological heuristic research study of the creation, development, and activities of the Magister Institute gathered information from interviews with five former Jesuits, including the researcher, and conversations with two current members of the Society of Jesus of the Antilles Province.

The outcome of this study is a composite depiction of Magister Institute as it evolved from a group of ten former Jesuits, was formally founded by six former Jesuits, developed and matured, and ultimately separated into two groups. The final individual depiction of events, personal implications, perceptions, and life experiences was gathered and synthesized. The researcher developed an overall synthesis and depiction providing explanations and understanding of the creation and establishment of this Institute.

The research methods and strategies are founded on the qualitative tradition of inquiry as they are interpreted and refined by the phenomenological heuristic research model. A six-step process commenced after the completion of the collection of the data. The six steps were as follows: initial engagement, immersion into the topic and question, incubation, illumination, explication, and creative synthesis. All of these steps were interconnected by means of dialogue. Basically, the researcher was actively promoting the other participants to rethink and make new judgments of the phenomenon under scrutiny after other points of view were accumulated and new syntheses re-drafted. According to Moustakas (1994), this interaction tends to elicit layers of depth and meaning, and ultimately helps improve more accurate depictions of the foundation of the Magister Institute. This return to the research participants brought to the study the necessary process of verification and rendered the understanding and consequent narrative of the phenomenon more accurate and reflective of reality as perceived by each of the participants. The researcher's expectation of more similitude at the end among the individual narratives was demonstrated, thus showing greater accuracy in depicting the creation of the Magister Institute.

This was a process of total immersion of the research participants and the researcher. The participant-observers were themselves founding members well as the researcher of this study. Since observation and leadership went hand-in-hand in this study, it was expected that the leadership style fostered member development in congruence with individual and group aspirations. The results of the study showed a greater perception of unity and group maturity in most of the members. The type of leadership used at different times and situations was described. Its effectiveness and relevance was also highlighted by means of a process of analysis and comparisons of the five different depictions based on a similar number of interviews. This special effort of comparing and sharing the opinions of the founding members, a true process of triangulation and member checking, acted as a guarantor of the rigor and trustworthiness of the study (Moustakas, 1994).

Rigor was increased in this phenomenological heuristic study not by contrasting other sources of information about the Magister Institute but by increasing the dialogue among the members participating in this study and by sharing information as it was being gathered in the process of data collection. Yet, the final synthesis was the responsibility of the researcher as he combined all different narratives and expressed them in their uniqueness and in their commonalities.

Philosophical Framework

According to Creswell (1998, 2005), the five main qualitative traditions were born in the 20th century. The first, dating back to 1989 was the *autobiography*, the second was *phenomenology*, the third *grounded theory*, the fourth *ethnography*, and the fifth, *case study*. Due to limitations in this research, the presentation will be limited to a brief description of phenomenology as related to this heuristic investigative study.

Phenomenology describes the meaning of lived experiences of groups of individuals in relation to one idea or phenomenon. Phenomenology has roots in the theoretical perspectives of several philosophers such as Husserl (1859-1938), Heidegger (1889-1976), Sartre (1905-1980), and Merleau-Ponty (1908-1961). Phenomenology has already had an impact on sociology, psychology, nursing and health sciences, and education. In this qualitative research methodology, two persons have been crucial in raising the level of acceptance of phenomenology by the dominant scientific community of their times: Carl Rogers (Hall et al., 1998) and Clark Moustakas (1994). These two authors made phenomenology move into a new level of acceptance in the scientific paradigm reigning at the time in the USA and Europe. They did this mostly through one concrete prevalent hard science of the times: Psychology. Rogers developed the union of scientific positivistic research with phenomenological investigations connected to Moustakas (1994), through the operational definition and the creation of important research tools like content analysis, rating scales, Q-technique studies, and experimental studies of the self-concept (Hall et al.). Rogers found a way to link phenomenological qualitative concepts to measurable, quantifiable, and predictable ones. This was a way to make qualitative research respected by the positivist scientists, prevalent in the scientific community of the American Psychological Association. Phenomenology has a history connected to Husserl, but it became accepted as real science only through the efforts of several contemporary scholars, including Moustakas, Rogers, and Swingewood (Creswell, 1998). The humanist psychologists used this method in conjunction with the operational definition, obtaining very creative intermediary steps between natural science and qualitative research (Hall et al.).

The following is a summary of procedural issues in using psychological phenomenology based on the interpretation of Creswell (1998). First, the writer tries to grasp the philosophical perspective of psychological phenomenology. The researchers then bracket all their preconceptions about the phenomenon to be targeted, through a construct called epoche, with the objective in mind of discerning the voices of the informants about the phenomenon from all other possible voices. Second, the writers develop questions to help clarify the meaning of the phenomenon for each participant or interviewee, asking these targeted persons for their lived experiences. Third, the investigators collect information from those with lived experiences related to the phenomenon. This data collection normally takes place through interviews and is augmented with their self-reflections and with the meaning extracted from the artistic works. Fourth, most psychological phenomenologists employ a similar series of steps. Usually the original protocol is divided into statements, a process called horizonalization. These units are then transformed into clusters of meaning, and these are articulated in psychological and phenomenological constructs. Fifth, these transformations are tied together to make a general description of the experience: the textural description of what was experienced, and the structural description of how it was experienced.

There are some considerations to be remembered before embarking on this type of psychological phenomenology. First, the phenomenological report helps the reader clarify the essence or invariant structure of the experience. Second, many persons find this type of research difficult because it requires a deep understanding of the philosophical rudiments of phenomenology. Third, the participants have had contact with the phenomenon. Fourth, researchers are to bracket personal experiences. Finally, it is up to the main writers or researchers to decide when and how their personal experiences are brought into the study (Creswell, 1998, 2005).

Methodology

This heuristic study exhibits several features involving psychological phenomenology. It was also based on several unique characteristics of the heuristic approach which distinguished it from psychological phenomenology.

While other approaches emphasize a certain distance from the phenomenon, heuristic studies recommend ongoing relationships and communication with the phenomenon under consideration.

Psychological phenomenology describes the structures of the experience, whereas heuristic research seeks to depict the personal meaning and significance of the phenomenon. Heuristic methodology leads to an act of synthesis, which in itself is also an act of creative discovery. In psychological phenomenology the research participants disappear after their descriptions and the essence of the structure of experience are complete. In this heuristic study, communication increased after the main depictions were submitted and further information from the depictions of other participants provided a basis for new dialogues. Psychological phenomenology describes the essence of the experience; heuristic phenomenology aims at describing the persons in their new context and experience. Heuristic research concentrates on the recreation of the lived experience from the frame of reference of the person who experienced it. Other narratives, documents, journals, diaries, or even dialogues complete and confirm the depiction. In this study, the researcher arrived at the final synthesis after following the six prescribed steps guaranteeing the purity and trustworthiness of the qualitative approach selected and recommended for this study.

The six-step process that began after the collection of the data was completed was comprised of initial engagement, immersion into the topic and question, incubation, illumination, explication, and creative synthesis. All of these were interconnected by means of dialogues. Basically, the researcher actively promoted the other participants to rethink and make new judgments of the phenomenon under scrutiny after other points of view were accumulated and new syntheses were redrafted. According to Moustakas (1994), this interdialogue achieves layers of depth and meaning, and in this case ultimately yielded more accurate depictions of the foundation of the Magister Institute. Returning to the research participants facilitated the necessary process of verification and made the understanding and consequent narrative of the phenomenon more accurate and reflective of reality as perceived by each of the participant members. The fact that there was more similitude at the end among the individual narratives demonstrated that they were all describing the creation of the same Magister Institute with greater precision.

This was a process of total immersion of the research participants and the researcher. The participant-observers were themselves founding members and one of their coordinators was also the researcher of this study. This is a good argument in favor of using heuristic phenomenology as the research method for this study (Moustakas, 1994).

Sample Selection

In general, qualitative research deals with a small number of people and goes deep into the situation and the perception or experience of the research participants (Creswell, 1998, 2005; Moustakas, 1990, 1994). There are several ways and procedures to choose the number of research participants, which is known as sample selection. The size of the sample and reasons for selection are explained and openly discussed (Creswell, 1998; Moustakas, 1990). The Magister Institute originally had six former Jesuits members of the ten former Jesuits who decided to meet and talk about their lives and their future. Four of them decided not to join the group, as it intended to consider common bases for apostolic work in common. The six founding members were considered as part of the sample. One of the members became incapacitated (Magister Institute collected papers, 2005), reducing the total possible choices and sample size of founding members to five out of a total of six. These five men were former Jesuits, ages between 54 and 68 at the time of the founding of the Magister Institute (Magister Institute collected papers, 2004). Two of them were ordained priests, three were psychotherapists, and two earned Ph.D. degrees. The five former Jesuits are educators, and three of them were involved during the founding of the Institute in teaching, administration, guidance and counseling services, and/or psycho-educational activities. The five members, former Jesuits, who founded the Magister Institute, are married with families. The other two members of the sample are two current Jesuits who have been in close contact with the creation and development of the Magister Institute. This sample was rich in experience and leadership endowments. The members' openness to discuss issues, friendliness, and mutual respect were conducive to arriving at descriptions and overall depictions of the phenomenon at hand. The study examined the leadership style of the Executive Committee including other core experiences in the development of the Magister Institute (Collected papers, 2004-2008). The five founding members were interviewed for a period of 45 to 60 minutes; the two current Jesuits were interviewed for a period of ten to twenty minutes. Their total time commitment did not surpass two hours.

Research Question

According to Creswell (2003), Patton (2002), and Yin (2003), qualitative research scientists are guided in their research by one or more questions. In phenomenology, these questions focus on the main question and help the researcher and participants to concentrate on the targeted phenomenon or special social event. In the Rogerian-Freirian interpretive paradigm, interviews could be focused on providing the rich and qualitative information necessary to achieve a complete and accurate depiction (Moustakas, 1990, 1994) using the leading power of the research questions selected.

The overarching questions served to focus the interview and related conversations during the entire process of the data collection and analysis. They also helped to reach the necessary consensus for the final creative synthesis.

According to Moustakas (1990, 1994), the overarching questions were described in very similar terms to those used by other major authors on qualitative research and phenomenological strategies (Creswell, 1998). There was one caveat in this comparison: the heuristic-phenomenological approach adopted in this study and especially this study's Freirian-Rogerian leadership style synthesis required a dialogical method and general attitude on the part of the researcher in relationships with research participants. This new style of relationship was such that interviews and conversations with the research participants looked more like a dialogue, an empathic mutual understanding, and a person-centered human interaction. In this light, the nature and intent of the subquestions following the overarching questions needed to be understood.

The overarching research questions were as follows:

> *What are your recollection/perceptions of your lived experiences in the creation and development of the Magister Institute?*

> *What are your recollections/perception of the leadership style of the Executive Committee in the creation and development of the Magister Institute?*

The following subquestions were presented as a stimulus and inspiration to help each research participant accurately describe a more comprehensive depiction of the phenomenon under scrutiny: the leadership style and processes including other personal and group experiences leading to the creation and development of the Magister Institute (Magister Institute collected papers, 2004-2009).

1. What, in your own words, are all the aspects of your feelings of separation from the Society of Jesus, as well as the experiences you have encountered with the religious and lay administrators of the Catholic Church?

2. What were the leadership strategies and any other ideas, feelings or emotions connected with the Society of Jesus that you consider most influential in the consolidation of the Magister Institute?

3. What were your fears and hopes for re-association with the Jesuits? What connection do you see between the leadership style of the Executive Committee and the reduction of your fears?

4. With the degree of success attained in the re-association of the former Jesuits of the Magister Institute with the current Jesuits in the Antilles Province, how much of this accomplishment do

you think is related to the leadership style of members of the Magister Institute?

5. What do you think are the possibilities of success of similar alternatives elsewhere in the Catholic Church? Given your experience at the Magister Institute, and the scarcity of Jesuits, what do you think of the interest shown by the Society of Jesus in re-associating with the former Jesuits to provide apostolic work? What are your thoughts about the degree and kind of re-association achieved between the current Jesuits of Miami, Florida, U.S.A., Dominican Republic, and Cuba, called the Antilles Province of the Society of Jesus, and the former Jesuits of the Magister Institute?

This was a study that offered key guidelines in an attempt to yield a phenomenological description of the personal experiences and observations of these men. The researcher selected five members of the Magister Institute who had direct lived experiences related to the development of the Magister Institute; and two current Jesuits who had a close relationship with the members of Magister Institute since its foundation. Heuristic phenomenological research strategies helped to understand what each participant in the research described as part of the experience of the "phenomenon" depicted, that is, the leadership style of the Executive Committee and the development of the Magister Institute, its purpose, achievements, and all related experiences connected with it.

Instruments

Like in qualitative research, the researcher became the main instrument responsible for data collection, organization, and analysis, and was the creator of the written reports of the findings (Patton, 2002; Strauss & Corbin, 1998). The researcher was nondirective and permissive in the dialogues and interviews, respected the uniqueness of each depiction and dialogue, and simultaneously, as Guba and Lincoln (1981) recommend, developed a global sense of the phenomenon.

MAGISTER: THE PHENOMENON OF MISSION AND
CAMARADERIE ROGERS-FREIRE FOR SOCIAL JUSTICE.

83

The immersion and incubation into the phenomenon leading to the illumination, the insight, and the synthesis that pooled everything together were necessary steps required of the researcher in utilizing the instrument of this research (Moustakas, 1990, 1994).

Role of the Researcher and Personal Bias

In accord with Creswell (1998, 2005), the researcher was of paramount importance in the planning and execution of this research study in the qualitative tradition. Several authors (Berg, 2001; Creswell, 1998, 2005; Patton, 2002) also recommended the selection of a single phenomenon as target of the investigation. All these authors consider that the concrete method within the qualitative tradition employed will determine the selection of strategies used in the process of data collection, analysis, and integration of individual depictions in one final overarching synthesis. The atmosphere created between the researcher and the interviewee fostered communication and mutual understanding, solid bases for a rich and sincere dialogue about the person's experience with the phenomenon (Moustakas, 1990). Several added characteristics were present in the interviewing process, given the training and experience of the researcher in nondirective interviewing and counseling: paraphrasing and inviting questions, adapting to the flow of the dialogues, refusing to allow his personal views and opinions interfere with the quality of reception and objectivity he owed to the information and ideas provided by the research participants (Creswell, 1998; Kahn, 1999; Rogers, 1963, 1967; Yin, 2003). The methods helped this researcher look at each opinion objectively and with utmost respect. The separate methodological processes were chosen and designed to guarantee objectivity and full attention of each participant. They included the open and clear acceptance of possible biases and the public decision to identify and suspend personal and possible biased judgments about concrete issues being considered immediately (Creswell, 1998, 2005). These processes to guarantee objectivity and respect of each participant were cautiously and watchfully observed.

This study encountered very few areas requiring the researcher's use of reflexivity, which is the most recommended strategy employed to handle successfully potential biases and possible predispositions (Johnson, 1997). An area of possible reflection dealt with the fact that the researcher is a member of the Magister Institute and has been with the group since its foundation as a member of the Executive Committee. This historical reality called for the phenomenological heuristic method of study, yet carried with it the possibility of not separating his experiences from those of the participants (Moustakas, 1990, 1994). Making this point public and recognizing its possible negative effects on the perception of events and their accurate interpretation provided a necessary and sufficient instance of critical self-reflection. The researcher, however, decided to take a second measure of protection against possible bias. Each person interviewed was contacted and presented with the researcher's personal interpretation of his depiction for amendment, embellishment, or rectification. This made the interviewees' descriptions and the researcher's depictions congruent.

The former Jesuits of this study, including the researcher, do not in any way harbor any antagonism towards the current Jesuits. They have crossed that bridge. This has been a study of the leadership strategies that helped the former Jesuits cross that bridge and the different experiences accompanying that journey. This means that, if after crossing all check points, some view has been expressed in a way that could be considered disrespectful, it was not a premeditated or ill-conceived act.

Data Collection and Processing Procedures

The common way of collecting information in heuristic research is through extended interviewing with an open and receptive attitude on the part of the interviewer. Moustakas (1990, 1994) and Rogers (1963, 1967) insist on the interviewer's capacity to generate understanding of all the issues dealt with in the interview from the frame of reference of the interviewee. They both agree that the creation of an atmosphere of freedom and empathic understanding

MAGISTER: THE PHENOMENON OF MISSION AND
CAMARADERIE ROGERS-FREIRE FOR SOCIAL JUSTICE.

85

is a prerequisite for the best information and communication to be exchanged in the interview. Moustakas (1990) mentions three main types of interviewing: the informal conversational, the general, and the standardized open-ended interview. He recommends the conversational, informal interview for its congruency with the rhythm and flow so typical of heuristic interviewing. Dialogue is recommended when freedom and empathic understanding are present (Rogers, 1969, 1977). The new interpretation of Rogerian person-centered communication that adds the element of fallibility to the dialogue and checks on it sporadically (Kahn, 1999) gives rise to Rogerian inspired interviews in the form of very spirited and dynamic dialogues. These dialogues are effective ways to discuss views of depictions after new information from the other interviews is being fed back to each of the research participants. This dialogue and conversational style inspired and evoked more accurate and all-inclusive depictions from each of the research participants, increasing trustworthiness and rigor of the depictions. As Moustakas (1990) so emphatically asserts, no one can plan a free flowing dialogue. The interviews and the following conversations and dialogues showed that openness and empathic understanding were present at all times. There were expressions from each member bearing witness to the presence of freedom and empathy in the conversations.

Guide of Procedures for Analysis of Data

The following is an outline of the procedures that were used for the analysis of data after the interviews were tape-recorded and transcribed (Moustakas, 1990).

1. Gathering all data from one research participant. The initial step of the organizing, handling, and synthesis-producing process was gathering all data from one research participant. This included the taped interviews, the depictions, notes about the participants, and document related to this research participant.

2. Immersion. This material was studied and analyzed, until it was thoroughly understood.

3. The first draft of the depiction. Here a period of rest was followed by one of intense study and analysis. Then codification and theme production was intensified. The first draft of the depiction was thus constructed. The language and the examples of the depiction were all from the individual research participant's experience of the phenomenon.

4. Back to the data to find congruence between the depictions already constructed. Since the raw data backed the description and the details selected from the depiction, the first case was temporarily finished.

5. Full revision. Since questions were raised and more time was required to reconcile the discrepancies found, a full revision was accommodated. This happened in the case of collaboration and in the case of choosing CLC as a community for the MI. This was resolved by dialogues and conversations between the researcher and each particular participant researcher.

6. The second case or research participant was undertaken following the same course of organization (Moustakas, 1990) and analysis as the first. This second case ended with an individual depiction that responded to the data gathered for the second research participant.

7. The depictions were ready. All individual descriptions were gathered together and reviewed following a systematic procedure: the main researcher proceeded to go intensely into the entire group of depictions and then took each one until he considered all parts (themes) of the phenomenon as described in these depictions were understood and made like a part of him. Here the commonalities and the idiosyncrasies were identified and assimilated by the researcher.

8. The first group depiction of commonalities and idiosyncrasies was thus developed. This depiction provided examples of descriptive accounts, narratives, conversations, illustrations, and

MAGISTER: THE PHENOMENON OF MISSION AND
CAMARADERIE ROGERS-FREIRE FOR SOCIAL JUSTICE.

87

other examples that helped reproduce the lively and dynamic spirit of the phenomenon.

9. The next step consisted of creating a common and most representative depiction of the entire group, by first using examples of the union of those depictions that best represented the entire group.

10. Finally, the researcher repeated the entire process and developed a fitting synthesis of the phenomenon. This final depiction was a product of study and analysis systematically carried out, but it was also a synthesis developed by the one most immersed in the depictions and responsible for the synthetic rendition of the individual and group depictions (Moustakas, 1990).

Standards of Quality and Verification

There were certain criteria that were congruent with heuristic research strategies in meeting the credibility gap, dependability, and confirmability. These criteria guaranteed a useful transferability of information.

Credibility

According to Krefting (1991), credibility requires submersion in satisfactory doses so as to be capable of identifying reappearing patterns, values, and themes. This approach requires submersion in the situation and, in this specific case, years of immersion in the same field of the interviewees' experiences. Familiarity with the research participants fostered richness of communication and quality of disclosure. This study increased its credibility through the use of member checking strategies as part of the research design, the expertise in the use of the nondirective techniques, and the use of reflexivity as part of the method of analysis and synthesis production.

Dependability

As Laura Krefting (1991) suggests, dense descriptions of research methods, triangulation and member checking, and peer examination were considered key elements in claiming trustworthiness or dependability of the study. Codification and themes sorting increased the credibility and dependability of the study, and these were essential parts of this study's methodology and procedure guidelines.

Confirmability

Some authors consider neutrality as data and interpretational confirmability. These authors do not view neutrality and objectivity as intimately interconnected (Lincoln & Guba, 1985). These authors look at the audit approach as the best way to authenticate confirmability. The heart of this strategy is directed to find the why and the how of the decision-making process. Going through this reverse process, from results to data, interpretations and synthesis provided the researcher with sufficient information to understand or at times even to arrive again at similar conclusions. This process is concentrated especially on the issues related to decision making, the why and how of each major step leading to results, interpretations, synthesis, inferences, data reductions, and data reconstruction. The audit strategy, according to Lincoln and Guba (1985) includes revision of six major categories: raw data (interviews), data reduction and analysis products, synthesis products, process notes, materials related to intentions and dispositions and the kind of information related to instrument development.

Since the Society of Jesus is considered rigorous, one of the largest and highly educated religious organizations of the Catholic Church (McDonough, 1998), the study was expected to provide interest and knowledge of the processes involved in the difficult, sensitive, and common transitions of religious members leaving their organizations. Major features of confirmability, according to Krefting (1991), were triangulation and reflexivity. Both were key ingredients of the research design of this phenomenologic heuristic study.

Transferability

The possibilities of this study to be applicable elsewhere depended on the credibility of its methods and its applicability mostly through the seriousness and academic competence of its researcher (Krefting, 1991; Moustakas, 1994). This can be deduced through the use of theoretical backing, methodological rigor, and transparency of the entire study. The passion of the exposition, the toughness of the arguments used, the clarity of the exposition of methods and research literature, and the power of the convictions exposed helped the reader and critic understand the depth of trustworthiness embedded in the narrative and exposition of this heuristic study.

Ethical Considerations

The ethical standards and guidelines of Barry University Institutional Review Board, also recommended by Creswell (1998, 2005) and Moustakas (1994), guided this study. The study conveyed the true findings in every area of research including interviewing, writing, analysis, and synthesis. Efforts were made to guarantee confidentiality at all times (Creswell, 1998, 2005; Denzin & Lincoln, 1998). Pseudonyms were used to protect the identity of interviewees. Separate storage facilities and appropriate safe boxes with locks were used to protect transcripts, audiotapes, and other potentially identifiable material. Consent forms approved by Barry University Institutional Review Board were used, appropriately explained and signed, and a copy given to all research participants. All documents assembled, including tapes, transcripts, and any other collected material have been stored safely. They will be protected for a period of 5 years, after which they will be destroyed.

Chapter Summary

This chapter presented a summary of the methodological strategies used in this study. The philosophical framework was discussed and both points of view, the quantitative and qualitative, were briefly explored. The traditions of qualitative research were also mentioned and phenomenology was more extensively discussed. The heuristic method was explained as a unique approach in itself, with specific distinctions from the psychological phenomenological approach. Clark Moustakas's suggestions were followed and his characteristic conception of the process of data collection was delineated. This approach was described as emphasizing ongoing communication between the researcher and the participants, and as respecting each participant's frame of reference and point of view. Participants and researcher have been described as arriving at a depiction of the phenomenon under study. Once the collection of the data was completed, six steps were followed until the final creative synthesis was concluded. The entire study was guided by two research questions, and clarified by several subquestions which helped the flow of the interviews. The sample selected was described and the interviewing process was explained. The role of the researcher as the main instrument of the study was briefly discussed. Finally, the topics of possible bias, credibility, dependability, transferability, confirmability and ethical considerations were presented and their relevance for this study was highlighted.

CHAPTER IV

RESULTS OF THE FINDINGS

Introduction

This is a study of the leadership style embedded in the creation and development of the Magister Institute. Originally, the former Jesuits met to discuss the possibility of engaging in some kind of apostolic work in common. In time, this unstructured group of ex-Jesuits, assisted by appropriate leadership strategies, moved from being distant and separate from the Jesuits to aspiring to become their collaborators.

The study explored the leadership processes that guided these men in their sincere search for their roots, identity, and a reoriented mission in life.

In qualitative research, focus and purpose are maintained by well-structured overarching research questions. This understanding is generally accepted by all qualitative research traditions of inquiry (Creswell, 1998). The overarching questions kept the interview and related conversations on course during the entire process of the data collection and analysis, and finally, helped reaching the necessary consensus for the final creative synthesis of the writing process.

The overarching research questions were as follows:

What are your recollections/perceptions of your lived experiences in the creation and development of the Magister Institute?

What are your recollections/perceptions of the leadership style of the Executive Committee in the creation and development of the Magister Institute?

The heuristic-phenomenological approach adopted in this study (Moustakas, 1990, 1994; Creswell, 1998) required a *dialogic method* and general attitude on the part of the main researcher in his relationship with research participants. This leadership style was such that the interviews and conversations with research participants resembled a *dialogue*, an *empathic mutual understanding*, and a *person-centered human interaction* (Moustakas, 1990).

In this research, a set of subquestions was also presented to the participants ahead of time with the objective of helping each of them prepare for the moment of the verbal depiction (the interview). These subquestions helped them to describe a more comprehensive depiction of the phenomenon under scrutiny (Appendix D). These sets of subquestions were not presented at the time of the interview to the research participants in order to provide them with the total freedom of an open-ended, non-directive, interviewing style

Demographics of the Participants

The group of former Jesuits who met and decided to discuss the possibilities of engaging in some kind of apostolic work in common was:

Originally made up of ten men.

All of them native of Cuba.

Ranging in ages from 50 to 67.

MAGISTER: THE PHENOMENON OF MISSION AND
CAMARADERIE ROGERS-FREIRE FOR SOCIAL JUSTICE.

93

They all knew most of the former and current Jesuits of the Society of Jesus pertaining to the Antilles Province (Dominican Republic, Cuba, Puerto Rico and Miami-Dade County, Florida, U.S.A.).

Several of them were close friends and classmates.

They all spoke English fluently, though their language used among themselves was always Spanish.

All of these ex-Jesuits had spent two to 20 years as Jesuits in training.

The original founding group was formed by six members. The sample is made up of the remaining five. This group has two priests, three with PhDs, and two with a Master's Degree in Education and Marriage and Family Counseling.

Findings: Themes

The interviews were taped and transcribed using only a code instead of the real name of each person. The researcher, following the guidelines of the heuristic phenomenological qualitative strategy, heard each taped interview and read the transcripts at least twice. After this intensive process of open and unstructured assimilation, another process of distance and resting was observed for two days after processing each transcript. Then again, a new process of analytical reading, making annotations on the margin of each of the transcripts, was initiated. These critical annotations were repeated at least twice until a revision of the entire set of transcripts was completed. After the annotations were completed, ideas, issues, and thoughts in any way connected to the overall research questions were tagged with descriptive codes. These codes and categories used were grouped and labeled. All this material was considered the "findings" of the study, directly coming from the analysis of the research participants' transcripts. Slowly all these codes and categories helped in subdividing the data or developing it into more inclusive and research-oriented units of meaning. These grouped units of meaning were slowly transformed into themes discovered through coding and analysis of the interviews. Six themes, finally, are presented here, based on the number of instances a theme was brought up by each of the participants and based on the relevance of the subject matter discussed. The key consideration for selecting a meaningful statement as part of a theme was its capacity for standing its own ground of meaning and illuminating an existing situation or its intimate association with one of the overarching research questions. Each research participant was identified by a number attached to MI. Thus research participants ranged from MI-1 to MI-7.

Theme 1: Camaraderie Among Former Jesuits

The former Jesuits recalled their Jesuit attraction and the fulfillment experienced in their shared commitment and sense of mission. MI-7 narrates his recollections this way: "This experience, lived in my college years, from my 18th to my 23rd year, in moments of great social and political tension in Cuba, from the year 1956 to the year 1961; those are the years in which I developed a decision of committing myself to join a group of men dedicating my life to carry forward a determined vision, a concrete way of feeling, and a unique way of thinking. All these things led me to enter the Society of Jesus."

MI-7 concentrates on his calling to the Society of Jesus: "Precisely, that same desire of connecting with others, of working in common, and complementing each other professionally, where each one contributed towards bringing forward a society that would be more coherent with the Christian vision: that of Jesus Christ." There is an element of emphasis in MI-7's vocation to the Jesuits: "With very few elements of what we could call the exceedingly pious and/or devotional type, I must say that 'Piety' in this external and overly sentimental way, was a collateral and almost irrelevant element in all my decision-making process. The fundamental emphasis was in human participation and sharing life together. This was for me, and continues to be, something that I am discovering a little more each time, the central point of my human vocation."

The experience of Magister awakens in the former Jesuits those dormant feelings of solidarity and shared mission in life. MI-7 describes his and the group's experiences this way: "From those initial encounters something was surfacing, which seemed dormant, but was there, inside me, always, and this was again that new desire of my adolescence, or of my first youth, my desire for that efficient solidarity to bring forth a vision of the Christian, Catholic, and Ignatian reality."

The new levels reached by this Magister experience are described by MI-2: "It is similar to what takes place in all institutions, the camaraderie that is produced between baseball, football, or basketball team players; those who go to war - the military - form a union with one another. Women have never understood why such a close friendship was developed between those who went to war, those who played football in college, or even those who have a career in common, such as doctors, dentists, or engineers." There is something special MI-2's experience has shown him about the camaraderie and selflessness built in stressful and unique situations: "The friendship, the respect, and the recognition that exists in a group that has been formed inside a segregated institution, with a series of rules- which at times are very harsh and difficult- because sport organizations demand teamwork, and teamwork demands that you sit down and allow someone else to play; that you learn that the objectives of the team are above the individual ones, and this forges a friendship and a bond of brothers."

The Magister camaraderie experienced is described by its founding members in very unique ways. MI-7 takes pride in providing this short depiction of the founding group of Magister that took place five years ago: "There are several important points specifically regarding the cohesion of the masculine group, who where the – let us call them – bonding members, because they were the connecting link between Magister and the Jesuits through their former experience in the Society of Jesus." MI-7 now describes with great sympathy and understanding the dynamics of communication of the founding Magister Institute: "And these are the characteristics: First, an affinity of the affective type, congeniality, a very special camaraderie, and an ability to treat one another with ease. Second, a vision, an intellect; in the fundamental factors, very much in common, there was a grand scale participation of intellectual understanding, which – logically – helped a great deal. But there was a community of thought and feeling, and this is what comes to mind of this experience. All had an enormous respect and love for the Ignatian vision of reality, similar to that of any Jesuit who would still be in the order."

MI-7 now turns to what according to him made this group's camaraderie possible, and a very important point to describe the leadership style of the Executive Committee: "Had it not been, nonetheless, in the case of some of us – myself included - for the orientation, enthusiasm, and drive of the original group, of the three who started this thing, the members of the Executive Committee, this would have not existed, it would have not taken place. That is, absolutely indispensably, a small group…as it is always… without Ignatius - since Javier would not have gone there - nor Pedro Fabro, Lainez, Salmerón, Rodriguez, or anyone else. That is, that this was absolutely necessary."

Magister was a group of former Jesuits whose ages ranged from 56 to 67 at its founding moments. This experience happened when former Jesuits were ranked matured persons, that is to say, not the normal age for group euphoria to take place. Again, MI-7 has the closing remarks: "However, I can say that despite our age then, and still now, it was a very youthful, creative and enthusiastic experience." The extraordinary way these older former Jesuits got along with each other was, according to MI-7 (personal dialogue after the interview) not to be compared with the experiences we had with similar Jesuit companions or the ones they have among themselves because we are standing on their shoulders. These experiences could not have taken place had we not lived the Jesuit way of life, and had we not experienced directly Jesuit camaraderie in its original fountain.

There is nostalgia in some of the founding members, reluctance to let these wonderful moments fade away. Can the founding members recapture them? Can they become a part of their ordinary existence? MI-1 says: "It is possible that this could have been, even, a yearning of something already lived, and something left behind, which they did not want to lose in order to have it - again - at hand, and take advantage of that past." MI-7, expresses these feelings well in the following paragraph: "In my case, remains something like a yearning for this to become a reality – which could happen again. A certain taste was left, the "after taste" we speak of in English, of those pleasant years in the past in which we shared insights. Those times were special and comparable to the historical and extraordinarily complex times we live in today. These are the times one becomes enriched with the visions and intuitions of others." MI-7 adds the following depiction of this Cuban classmates' dream team: "This group is an eminently intuitive group; after all it is a Cuban group, quite witty. That is something one yearns for and is not easily found anywhere, nor is it found on the newspaper, nor in other human groups, not even in the family. It is found in this group; truly a rare gathering of people whose heads light up with rare "bulbs" and have ideas. That is yearned for."

There is an element of sadness when one realizes that what took place five years ago and reached a peak; now is like in a state of "wait and see." This feeling, together with the others of mission, education, and apostolate are mixed and well expressed again by MI-7:

"Fundamentally, it is a desire of, good heavens, how sad that things could not take place just as we had wished; but, if it was not quite complete it was not because it could not have been done, rather because there were certain limitations not taken into consideration, and the situation was not handled in the proper manner. Or, perhaps, the difficulties were greater than our dreams. But, what remains is that desire, the delight of being able to share, for most of those who are in this group, the experiences and visions that we consider a little bit like the culmination of what one has been able to experience in life." The following descriptions of MI-7 will capture something so unique to the former Jesuits' group as contrasted with the non-Jesuit members: "we wish we could transmit it, transfer it and communicate it to another group, even a younger group, be it directly through a small community, or through other individuals to whom we become closer with the intention of sharing life, even when they have not been members of a determined apostolate of any kind." Some reflection perhaps might be in order, as MI-1 succinctly states: "Then, in some way, there is a yearning and a desire to see what you truly received in the past, and how you took advantage of it. And, according to that, get together and share those past experiences, in such a way that they may be actualized."

MI-1 offers a closing remark while emphasizing the importance of lived experiences and quiet listening to the call summoning each one from the heart and mind of each other: "that you may reunite with your past and your present. It seems to me that this is important, especially after many years, after you have made personal contact and – in some way – feel summoned and called by one another."

Theme 2: Attraction/Mistrust: Intertwined Feelings towards the Jesuits

The second theme that was selected among the ones found in the different interviews is the *attraction/mistrust* that most of the time seems to be intertwined in the former Jesuits' expressions. MI-6 tells the good side of this relationship former Jesuits-current Jesuits, with the following words: "In terms of the Society, yes, I emotionally remember many memories with great fondness… And then, the spirituality, the formation, and the whole environment that Ignatian spirituality and formation build inside a group of men committed to do something for Christ."

Each of the former Jesuits had admiration toward the Jesuits as a given, dating back to the origins of that relationship. MI-6 continues with the story: "Because there is something I say to Fr. Aleman: 'Do you know why is it that I have come to the conclusion that I do not have a vocation? I certainly did want to have the vocation to the Society of Jesus. However, if I could ask God for something at this moment it would be to have this vocation, because what I would really like to be was a Jesuit…But, I thought I was not going to be a good Jesuit; because I was not able at the time.' Then, at that moment, he stopped me and told me 'leave'." There is a sense of looking up to the Jesuit way of living and together a contradictory feeling of leaving the Order; a sense of relief and freedom in becoming a married lay man jointly with a growing sense of admiration for the Jesuits now distant. MI-6 makes a point about these two contradictory feelings he found competing within himself still months and years after he left: "However, I believe that it took a lot from me and years in order not to constantly be an internally divided person… but, how to be able to reconcile the dream of being a Jesuit with the reality of becoming a layman, married, with children." A voice of reason and reflection invites the former Jesuits to study and analyze the Jesuit experiences and compare them with the ones each one of the former Jesuits have been involved with since their separation from the Order. This is MI-1 expressing it his way: "I am not certain to what degree you currently feel satisfied of your past and the decision you made; perhaps, it is now that you have become crudely aware of what you have lived and what you are now living, after so many years. Then, that served as motivation and, at the same time, as an invitation to reunite, to share and formalize something that would help them to truly recapture and take advantage of the past experiences along with the actual ones."

One key feeling all the former Jesuits express in their recollections is rejection. MI-2 explains the feeling this way: "It is not easy for an institution, as would be, not only the seminary…but also an institution such as the police, the army, the marines, the French Legion…it is not easy for them as a body, as an institution, to see with grace those who have abandoned the institution." This feeling is expressed by all, and is understood as part of normal life, something one cannot change and must accept. MI-2 explains this experience with a graphic and sad story: "That is, in a way, a basic principle applied to all institutions, and much more so to one of this type, which is a religious career with a specific vocation; when one left the seminary fifty years ago, one was hidden and taken through a door during the cover of night so that no one could see him. They would leave him on the streets without a cent in his pocket, and practically what took place was close to a funeral, stating 'so and so left,' which was to say 'he died'… everyone's faces belonged in a funeral parlor."

These experiences that we all had, touching directly some of us, or touching a close friend of us, give MI-2 sufficient information to make the following prediction: "The original idea, which at least occurred to me during the first meeting, that the Jesuits were not interested in accepting the ex-Jesuits, that idea – in my opinion – has not changed." This is something that has withstood time, five wonderful years of Magister relationships and five years of dreaming to be accepted. MI-2 rethinks the depth of this statement and changes it this way: "But, completely accepting the contribution of a group, such as the Magister Institute that was willing to cooperate without financial recompense to the institution of the Jesuits that, still today, has not been completely accomplished – in my opinion." Another founding member of Magister has the following recollection of similar feelings: "I remember one of us who militantly did not wish to have anything to do, or in any way place himself under any type of authority that had to do with the Jesuits. It seems to me that there was another who – not so passionately, because he had always maintained a relationship with the Jesuits - structurally, if I remember correctly, showed certain reluctance to a formal connection, however always fostered dialogue with the Jesuits." MI-2, very realistic and matter of fact in his statements, brings out a basic pedagogic Jesuit principle consisting in making the necessary changes in you, which are under your control, to face the out of your reach realities of life. MI-1 thinks that through ascetics and personal growth former Jesuits can attain cohesion, maturity and become ready for collaboration at its proper time:

> Respecting the characters in the personalities, what has taken place, the family, the children, the influential circumstances, the reasons behind making decisions and also the reasons – at this moment – to be able to see everything from one's personal perspective. Then, I truly

MAGISTER: THE PHENOMENON OF MISSION AND CAMARADERIE ROGERS-FREIRE FOR SOCIAL JUSTICE.

101

believe that it is a good experience, very beneficial, and I think that, respecting the characters, the personalities, and the reactions of each individual, of one group as much as the other, and after certain division which seems natural after the formation received; therefore, take advantage of this time and truly become aware of your lives, of your past and present, so that you may analyze it profoundly.

The entire group of founding members has these feelings intertwined, with a subconscious, ready to jump out, hope of acceptance and sincere collaboration with the Jesuits. MI-2, who has been so open in sharing feelings of frustration and realism, closes this section with a final note of hope: "And it is possible that in a not so distant future a new Father General may have an ample and different attitude and send out an order that may be embraced with fervor and change this underlying tension." One can read the feelings and the expectations embedded in this note or message-in-a-bottle. Former Jesuits, after one reviews their transcripts and conversations are still waiting. Currents Jesuits, after one reviews their interviews and conversations, are seen as hopeful, waiting, individually receptive, and hoping for a better overall collaboration effort.

Theme 3: The Identity of Magister: CLC and ACU

The origins of MI are narrated by MI-3 highlighting the fact that a non-directive approach was used to allow the former Jesuits to freely and openly lead their own way. MI-3 remembers: "I believe that it all started as an abstract restlessness, rather exploratory, a restlessness of former Jesuits to do something in common, or to get to know each other, or visit one another. You started it, as I remember it, definitely, without any anticipated structure." MI-6 describes his first reactions to the invitation to meet with other former Jesuits: "I took it with great enthusiasm. I wanted to respond to that in a very positive manner and, of course, it looked to me something very well presented by you and I felt very comfortable with the idea."

He continues the narration telling about the questions raised in him by the invitation: "And I had many questions inside of me. And these questions were, primarily, addressing the idea of how people in general would react to this proposal. At the time, I had no knowledge of any attempt that this could have existed or that someone could be actually doing it." The next citation from MI-6 touches upon a very important vocational element, the former Jesuits felt a call coming from other former Jesuits to gather in this group or community: "Nevertheless, it looked to me as a challenge. It looked like something in need of an answer."

MI-1 makes this mutual calling a central point of the maturity and healthy psychological independence of Magister: "In some way, to be able to feel summoned and called by one another." This first experience of the former Jesuits is told by MI-6:

In this regard, I think I have more or less described what at the beginning could have given continuity to the Ex-Jesuits group. It was that great interest for the things of St. Ignatius and for the Society. It has been said before that we did not want to become Jesuits again. By the way, I did not like the name of 'ex-Jesuits'. I didn't feel as an 'ex-Jesuit'. I felt like a man with a great conviction about the Spirituality of St. Ignatius.   You can call this what you want, but I have had a common experience with these other men about what we thought the Society (of Jesus) was. But, I really believe that overtone was clear enough in this regard. Even the ones that left were also clear in regard to the fact that no one pretended that we create a Jesuit fantasy.

From another angle, MI-7 describes the basic elements he saw in the convening group of former Jesuits. These meetings awoke in this group of friends a new dimension and a new dream: "The periodic meetings start with that general attitude, and I must express that - little by little - it began to reappear, a vision started to form, a humble desire to place the talents of that small group, which at the time was formed by four or five, to function, so that this communion of visions could produce some fruit, etc., in the society we lived. The reunions turned out to be pleasant, there was a congenial dimension, happy, communitarian, affective, and the directors, coordinators – the three 'heads,' to say so – and the coordinator carried the reunions effortlessly, with ample freedom for everything, helping us -who where there - to feel much at ease."

The founding or core-group of Magister was, according to the depictions of its members, a sort of "dream team." The group had the levels of camaraderie very high, as it was described. The group was ruled by consensus and each opinion counted. The founding members had a common Jesuit formation and life style as so eloquently MI-5 notes: "It seems to me that the formation of the Magister Institute is an excellent idea, because it is formed of well prepared individuals, all with a basic idea of an education inside the Society of Jesus. It is true that they lived in different times, in dissimilar places, but there is a basic matrix of things that have been learned, such as study habits, habits of certain honesty and certain fidelity, as well as certain homogeneity of criteria."

Magister as a core-group of former Jesuit men lasted close to one year of intensive meetings, communication and spiritual sharing. This formative experience has been recalled by each of the founding members. MI-7 summarizes the memories and the nostalgia: "There are several important points specifically regarding the cohesion of the masculine group, who where the – let us call them – founding members, because they were present, there, through their experience in the Society of Jesus. And these are the characteristics: First, an affinity of the affective type, congeniality, a very special camaraderie, and an ability to treat one another with ease. Second, a vision, an intellect; in the fundamental factors, very much in common, there was a grand scale participation of intellectual understanding, which – logically – helped a great deal." MI-7 tries to describe the group's cohesiveness and common grounds: "But there was a community of thought and feeling, and this is what comes to mind of this experience. All had an enormous respect and love for the Ignatius vision of reality, similar to that of any Jesuit who would still be in the order."

The motivations that led the group to increase its size and bring in the wives as a next step in its planned development were fairly clear.

The first to comment on this new road is MI-1, who speaks through the voice of experience: "Then, it seems to me, that you moved forward too fast, wanting to organize something without thoroughly considering the desired outcome, without becoming identified in the matter; you wanted to invent, create something new, like an ideal – which seems good to me – but, I think that you moved forward too fast following your desire to organize and form an organic body without it having the maturity to become one." MI-1 is referring to the fact that Magister brought in their wives and several other couples reaching its number to 19 in two months. MI-4 tells the story: "Magister grew to become the largest CLC of South Florida; but like in a hurry without calculating the possible consequences." There were several issues involved in this move. One, it seems that the group wanted to be accepted as lay people, and no more as ex-Jesuits, as MI-6 states: "But perhaps we felt like missing an organizational identity. In other words, it was not enough to us. We could talk among ourselves; we could identify ourselves very well. However, we felt we could not introduce the group as such to no one and say 'this is this'."

"It became a hot issue at the time" as MI-4 recalls, "to become lay members of the Church and to get rid of the 'ex-Jesuit' label that defined us in a negative fashion." MI-6 clears this point saying: "Because the idea came about that what is it that we are, and then we say: 'we are lay persons, we cannot keep identifying ourselves as ex-Jesuits'. It was a negative definition. Then, in order not to define ourselves in a negative form (ex-Jesuits), we wanted to positively define ourselves, and positively we were lay men. All of us, we were ten lay men."

The members of the Executive Committee tried to create a model of a group according to the ideals and expectations of the group and did two things. One, according to MI-3: "Immediately, visited the Internet and downloaded the definition of a Christian community. With this new realization came a change, which I believe became an institutional point of maturation at the time, since we were looking for what we wanted to do with our desire to help, our desire to improve, and our desire to share a friendship then, as well." Actually, it is MI-3 the only one who saw this move, at the distance of five years, as an institutional maturity step. MI-6, on the other hand, tells the story this way: "My impression and this is going to sound somewhat strange, is that we took the wrong turn. We were in a hurry without the need to be so, because we did not have to go to any particular place and be there at any particular time. What we really had to do was to solve a problem. It looked like someone was waiting for us to give some form to something that didn't have any. What we were looking for was something else. Nevertheless, when the CLC organization model was presented to us, the group thought that, all of the sudden, we have found the solution to the problem. The group was mesmerized by this concept."

MI-6 sees this move as a mistake that the group made without any reason to do it. He also brought to this discussion the fact that the group already had planned to define itself and had written By-Laws and General Principles. Says MI-6: "Not only that, but we dedicated significant time to work on rules and regulations for the Magister Institute. However, there we were describing an organization that had nothing to do with the CLC. In other words, we were describing an educational and socially oriented association which had no relation to the CLC whatsoever." According to MI-6 this mistake was avoidable and no one of the group stepped forward and helped the others see the point. On the other side, MI-3 thought this was the correct move and gave arguments to solidify his selection: "I remember that I argumented, at the time, that this would give us a theological or formational background, because there was an Internet, there were documents, there was affiliation where it could be projected and inserted in an existing body, which – at the very least – shared our spirituality, because it was, after all, a Jesuit community of Christian life. Then, in a way, I believe that it was very natural, we all agreed and moved forward with the affiliation."

MI-6 grants the argument that all the core-group made the move thinking they all had reached a moment of "institutional maturity" and future stability. MI-6 says it very sharply: When we got enthused with the CLC format and understood that it was a quick and comfortable way to become operational; it called our attention and the CLC charisma captivated the group. I think that what happened was that we saw things, which seemed to be similar to what we were seeking, but they were not the same thing. I think it was like I had commented before that it was something already made and comfortable. We did not have to create something which would have taken much more effort, so we went that way. What we really did was to investigate what was the CLC movement; and how the CLC was functioning and, more specifically, operating right here in Miami.

MI-3, who recognized being the great sponsor of the CLC transition and transformation, started realizing the immediate consequences of the move. Several couples were invited to become members by one of the members of the EC. The group increased, counting all the wives of the former Jesuits, up to 19 members. "At the same time, I believe that even though this was one of the strengths of the Magister, consequently, it became a difficulty, in the sense that – in a way - it became a subgroup; since they were accustomed, for years, to go out and eat, and so on, it was very easy for them to come to an agreement that was not necessarily shared by others in the group who were not a part of the group of friends." He is mentioning something that happened, as MI-4 tells us: "One of the members invited a very professional and mature group of couples, very close friends of him and his wife. They became about half in size the number of the entire group. Now we had two new issues to deal with, our wives and the non-Jesuit subgroup of one of the founding members. All had happened without anyone of the founding members realizing it happening." MI-3 also very sincerely and critically recognizes that this incoming group had brought also some difficulties with them: "Even though it was a strength, because it rapidly increased everything and all, it was also – in a way – a point of division, since those who were not in the subgroup may not have had the time, the manner, or the history to be able to achieve a common vision, while for the others it was easy to find a common vision of what they wanted to do or what it seemed right to them, so certain difficulties began to emerge." MI-3 continues with his insightful description of what happened after Magister became a CLC and the group reached 19: "Also, another source of disunion, and where I believe the leaders became divided as well, was in the nature of the group we wanted to form. I believe that

MAGISTER: THE PHENOMENON OF MISSION AND
CAMARADERIE ROGERS-FREIRE FOR SOCIAL JUSTICE.

107

the group of Johnny and his friends seemed to have a more emphatic type of group, as they used to have, in their friendship to us; they did not wish to exclude us in anything, but the friendship... whereas we would go out to eat, perhaps prayed a little together, and perhaps shared a little formation, but it would be as a soft way of sharing life." This interpretation of MI-3 has become the one accepted already by the founding members, as they expressed in these descriptions. MI-4 clarifies the issue:

The group, with the addition of our wives became involved in discussions and explanations that we never had before. With the full addition of the non-Jesuit members, three couples, the group had deep and varied formations needs and little intellectual cohesion and single-mindedness. Some of the new members, right from the beginning, were not in accord with the rest in many simple matters, like respect for each other, interfering in the group process by jumping ahead of others to speak their mind, and non-acceptance of the concept of mission, apostolic activities and social justice works. The group was going through a difficult time, and thanks to the common sense, mutual respect and admiration prevalent among the founding members, the group survived major disorders and moved on to a new viable situation for all.

There were some immediate changes in the life and spirit of Magister. The founding members have come with analysis of what happened in a unanimous manner, at least in the final interpretation and possible outcomes. MI-6 tells of changes in the leadership style as applied to the entire community, composed of former Jesuits, wives of former Jesuits, and members who were not former Jesuits: "Did the leadership change? Well, the process of leadership changed. Because things could not be any more like it was at the beginning when men were the only ones. Things were said, were understood, were developed, and there was great respect for each other's opinion. All this was modified by a position represented by an attitude of 'Let us do this... We must do this.' And, many times the group process was not of a dialogue to rapidly arrive to a consensus, but rather an interactive argument."

MI-4 brings here a historical perspective: "My leadership style was elaborated among the founding members. It was the ordinary way of relating to each other. Non-directive leadership, management by consensus, group of equals' style of leadership, all these are terms to describe the original Magister Institute leadership style of leadership. Now, with the group so divided, and the expectations so fractioned, only a major meeting of the leaders who created and developed this magnificent group could stop the bleeding, help the reconstruction, and produce a working solution that at least would bring the peace to all, and let time come to help with an appropriate evaluation and new lights of hope and never ending former Jesuit tenacity, sense of mission and camaraderie. I think these interviews, open ended and sincere will point the way toward the future." Again a voice of experience, MI-1 leaves his advise: "It seems to me that all that created frictions, created jealousy, produced the anticipation of who was going to be in charge and how far the authority of the coordinator would reach and the authority of those who would be added to the group. Then, all that contributed to the creation of things without maturation, moving forward too fast, desiring to organize something that still needed maturity and discernment. This way, things would fall by their own weight, and the experience would include not only the personal but also the group level.

MI-7 brings here a delicate, all-encompassing vision and evaluation of the entire process Magister went through: "Later, firmly believing that something beautiful could come out of that, uniting different professional characteristics and specialties, etc., perhaps, we could say that the Christian Life Community model was probably the closest to what the existing members wanted to do and held at hand; however, it was, a system already established, in which – perhaps – the vocation of the group could not be fully satisfied."

MI-7 tries to compare the simple experience of the former Jesuits when alone, by themselves, with a new experience when in couples: "But, forcing that experience, that very masculine experience, our experience, with this grand ease and adaptability, and even the capacity of differing from one another and - at the end - joyfully hugging one another, etc., when the matrimonial element was added, the nature of the complete issue changed. Because now it was almost as if the member was not the individual, but the couple."

MI-6 insists that the group went the wrong way looking for psychological support: "But, we wanted -and I think we did it psychologically because we had the immense need of support. However, we went to look for it to the wrong place; we went to the CLC."

MI-4 brings here an argument that can be put together with MI-1's central issue: "Magister, the founding members, did not need to become CLC, we needed no collaboration with the Jesuits to give meaning to our apostolic commitments, we just needed to trust in ourselves deeply and let the Spirit guide us, in a simple way, with open and sincere hearts, to continue the work we started in such a beautiful and fulfilling way. I, for one, think that difficulties will not stop this founding group from continuing the work begun and the friendship reestablished. There is space for forgiveness and room for hope in our hearts and minds. That is my optimism." Again the voice of wisdom and experience MI-5 leaves his message: "But, it seems to me, that the idea of the group was a good one, and the group is still in the process of becoming, one may say. There may have been some separations, etc., but I believe that, in general, it has given a positive fruit, and in the future, when some of the harshness that may have taken place, etc., can be honed, the group will function with greater cohesion, with a unified criterion of objectives and stratagems, and also of strategies for the short and long run."

The group is divided because, according to MI-6: "There is a sub-group of the ex-Jesuits who very much insist in having a mission. But, there is another bigger group who did not understand at the moment what a mission was. But, this is very idiosyncratic to the way of being of the Jesuits and, consequently, of the Ex-Jesuits attending the meeting. Why? Because lay people are used to thinking more in terms of prayer-group-mentality."

A group within the major group was already experiencing discomfort and showing discontent when certain topics were discussed. MI-6 makes the following assertion: "For example, the group felt very united whenever we were having prayer and formation. But, when the topic of mission would come about, I could perceive in people's faces a profound concern." MI-4 again puts things in perspective:

It seems that all the former Jesuits and several of their wives, together with one couple also made up of one former Jesuit, though not a founder of Magister, and one single lady also a professional, all these members' spirituality was centralized in the concept of mission, and their concept of prayer was also intertwined with apostolic work (contemplation in action). This meant that the division concerning mission was not quite down the middle. There were other issues at stake here. Organization, rules, discipline, mutual respect, and sharing a common vision and understanding, were also part of discussion.

MI-2 thought that the seed of future division was planted early in the group as so many persons were allowed to be part of it without any criteria of acceptance: "I think that despite the extraordinary effort of those who directed the institution, to keep the peace, the calm and the objectivity, the destructive forces were much greater than the constructive forces." The reality of the group situation continued, and MI-4 brings historical evidence to the fore in this crucial moment: "The way our groups separated from each other was not a simple thing. It was a matter also of old friendships involved and the lack of resolve of some members to be ready to offer themselves for some apostolic activity." The group was becoming two separate entities and the leadership of the founding members was concerned. MI-6 narrates his perception of the process: "Right there, I saw the beginning, not only of a crack in the cohesiveness of the group but in the group communication. Communication began to deteriorate because we started to see more arguments and discussions going nowhere; leading to nothing concrete, elevating the level of frustration."

This situation continues to deteriorate. Leadership is of one kind among the former Jesuits and it is completely different when dealing with the entire group. This changes the style of leadership to the extended-MI community. MI-6 captures this moment of bitterness and misunderstanding in the following depiction: "Then, this process changed the leadership style. Right there and then, leadership was directive with minimal participation. There were some who did not participate in practically anything. Individuals who seemed to be very comfortable being there, yet they would not say a word."

The moment was one of tension and something had to be done at the leadership level. MI-4 brings information to the open not known before and yet capable of being confirmed: "Magister was founded through a group effort and team of equals' approach. Yet, this effort and this approach had two persons, at times three, behind providing facilitation and motivation for expectations in each one, and never crossed the lines of telling anybody what each one of them had in mind for the entire group." MI-4 threw some light into these chaotic moments: "These two founding members knew each other since the beginning of High School and had worked together as college professors in two occasions." MI-4 continues: "These two main persons always remained on top of the facilitation processes of the entire group and the subgroup. This difficult situation was interpreted by them as dangerous and in need of special efforts on their part. The two of them met in the library of the Seminary to discuss the immediate future of Magister in a serious and decisive way. Each one expressed his sincere vision of the situation. A decision was reached by consensus. You go your way with the subgroup and we go our way with the original founding group of former Jesuits." Up to here the necessary elements were discussed and quickly agreed, a sign of that quick communication style based on understanding so many times brought up by the founding members in these depictions. MI-4 makes the final remarks clarifying unknown details of this difficult separation: "We promised to keep in touch and never allow anything to interfere with our long friendship and common vision. Then he stood up and acted in a decisive way, and I, the other one, did the same. Since that time, two groups were formed who backed each other and who never argued again. Peace was permanent. Non-directive leadership, with a touch of Paulo Freire's radical pedagogy put the two groups in separate environments and has kept the faith and the hope alive."

Finally some comments were provided from the founding members in relation to the past, a sort of an evaluative summary. MI-6 makes the following reflection:

> What would you have done, in order to avoid what actually happened? Well, first of all, we should have never joined the CLC. We should have continued our search looking for our own organizational format. We should have had the courage to say 'Let's create our own organization, something like an Institute, Magister Institute'. And, we should have started this idea, and we should have been like a lantern that would have illuminated this path, and we should have allowed ourselves the freedom to speak our minds. Right there and then, we lost the right path.

This means that according to MI-6 the group with a vocation to follow and continue is the one made up of founding members. But he emphasizes that the group with vocation had to be clear of interferences and must reassemble and remain cohesive and of one mind. The fact remains that the MI became a CLC and the wisdom of this decision has been questioned by several founding members. MI-7 sees this situation this way: "Though the Christian life communities were the closest to the pursued ideal, however, they did not reach it completely; the other alternative would have been to have created something new, different, simple and without great aspirations, but made a bit closer to the measure of the circumstances, and this did not take place."

According to MI-4 "the group actually added the wives, then the other couples of non-Jesuits and finally split in two, the original group of former Jesuits and the subgroup of non-Jesuits, roughly speaking. The group of former Jesuits evolved from one, cohesive, simple group of former Jesuits with a set of bylaws individually and thoughtfully made by the founding members through a steering committee of their own choosing." These are explanations coming from sources that up to now have kept "silence and calm" as the only answers. MI-4 adds these few

remarks to make this stage of Magister slightly more understandable:
"The wise decision we all agreed to live by consisted in keeping in
touch, calling activities off, and waiting. Websites call this interim
stage 'currently under construction', electrical and cable companies
use the terms 'will be back shortly.' Right now it seems that things are
beginning to connect again. Can difficulties outweigh our capacity and
tenacity to remain united and follow our original dream?" MI-7 looks
back at the experience of the former Jesuits and thinking about the
future makes the following evaluative comments: "In my case, remains
something like a yearning for this to become a reality; that this could
happen again." Then looking back says:

> A certain taste was left, the 'after taste' we speak
> of in English, of those pleasant years in the past,
> sharing insights, even more so *in* such historical and
> extraordinarily complex times as the ones we are
> living today - when one becomes enriched with the
> visions and intuitions of others; and this group, is an
> eminently intuitive group, after all Cuban, quite witty.
> That is something one yearns for and is not easily found
> anywhere, not found on the newspapers, or in other
> human groups; not even in the family. It is only found
> in this group; truly a rare group of people whose heads
> light up with unusual 'bulbs', and come up with new
> ideas. That is yearned for.

MI-7 writes with emotions and a critical understanding when
accepting that there were some limitations the group did not know how
to handle in an adequate manner: "Fundamentally, it is a desire of, good
heavens, how sad that things could not take place just as we had wished
and planned; but, if it could not reach completion it was not because it
could not have been done, but rather because certain limitations were
not properly taken into consideration, and the situation was not handled
in a suitable way. Or, perhaps, the difficulties were greater than our
dreams." MI-7, an original former Jesuit brings forth that imbedded

sense of mission and service they all had: "But, what remains is that
desire, the delight of being able to share, for most of those who are in
this group, the experiences and visions that we considered a little bit like
the culmination of what one has been able to experience in life; and we
wished we could transmit it, transfer it and communicate it to another
group, even a younger one, be it directly through a small community, or
through other individuals to whom we become closer with the intention
of sharing life, even when they have not been members of a determined
apostolate of any kind." MI-7 is very conscious of the age factor in
this group: "Also, something that we would have to keep in mind, and
logically we must keep in mind, is the age of the group, the average age
of that group, of the men, at least. There was not one less than 55 years
old. That colors and shades this experience in a very special manner.
I do not think that there have been many institutions in the history
of humanity, specifically of Christianity, where that phenomenon has
taken place as far as the emergence of something truly significant during
that period of life." MI-7, when mentioning the age factor, immediately
corrects himself: "However, I can say that despite our age then, and
still now, it was a very youthful, creative and enthusiastic experience."
MI-6, in a very emphatic way concludes: "We should have looked for a
more precise vision and be better aware of what we really wanted first.
We should have met and said: We do not need money, organizations,
or structures. We need nothing of that sort."

MI-7 still wants to make the point of the identity and uniqueness
of the Magister Institute's quest:

> The fact of the existing mold of the Christian life
> community, instead of creating one adapted to the
> circumstances, because these are very exceptional
> circumstances, even when there are many things in
> common with the Christian life community. Someone
> would say: no, but there could be a peculiar Christian
> Life Community, with its liberties and such...Yes, but
> what comes first, the peculiarity or the Christian Life
> Community? I would prefer to say that ours is something

MAGISTER: THE PHENOMENON OF MISSION AND
CAMARADERIE ROGERS-FREIRE FOR SOCIAL JUSTICE.

115

very peculiar and that, good heavens, it seems to have some likeness with a Christian Life Community, but this is already an *a posteriori judgment*. This is already a Christian Life Community and then we will see how the peculiarities of this group can fit in. It seems to me that things do not function this way.

MI-6, MI-7, MI-2 and MI-4 have competed with each other to express their vision of a simple and most unique organization made up of only former Jesuits. MI-3 had the same vision of Magister as unique and 'group of equals' though he does not see contradiction with becoming a CLC organization. MI-1 and MI-5 do not touch this issue in their depictions. MI-4 makes the final remark:

MI-3 was always a defining force in the direction of group of equals' leadership style and has always considered that Magister could not reach its full realization until the subgroup had separated from the former Jesuits and until both groups had followed their special charisma. MI-3 holds that mission and community service are 'non negotiable essential parts of our vocation and charisma.' It is very likely that, with forthcoming dialogues among the former Jesuits, these clarifications will facilitate the much needed common understanding among Magister members.

There is a final point that MI-7 brought to clarify the identity of the MI. He is the only one who compares the efforts of Magister with those of the CLC and simultaneously with the ACU. MI-4 offer some help to see the point of this comparison: "The ACU, Agrupación Católica Universitaria, is one outstanding example in the Hispanic world of a different model of organization of lay men working in close collaboration with the Jesuits. The ACU model has become somehow obsolete because the CLC movement has tried to change the concept of these organizations of lay men and women closely associated with the

Jesuits all around the world. Yet the former Jesuits have an important thing to say about this experience with the CLC and the way they see still today the model of ACU." MI-7's depiction might be the most graphic of the examples:

> The ACU is a much closer model. I believe that had the ACU been open to accept, with all the logical requirements of the community, individuals who have gone through the experience of exiting the Society of Jesus, it would have been a good experience to take example from, but I believe that still an internal maturity is required for that, including cultural factors, which are not easy within the Hispanic culture. The distinctiveness of the   ACU could help in the sense of the masculine, and a vision that is not quite similar to that of the Christian life communities, on one hand; on the other hand, the ACU offers also an experience of a community that was created *ad hoc* at the moment of its inception, specifically with the urgency of an existing need.

MI-7 continues:

> In that sense, the ACU model would be helpful since something specifically *ad hoc* could be designed here, rather than adjusting and accommodating to pre-established structures and/or statutes. Truly, it is a *sui generis* experience, very special, very unique. The ACU, however, has a very strong presence of a director, and ours would require a different balance and equilibrium in the distribution of authority, it would be something of a more participatory nature with much more community decision making, and a more mature conception of the style of life. Since its inception, the ACU conceived the director as a basic and central figure, such as the one

MAGISTER: THE PHENOMENON OF MISSION AND
CAMARADERIE ROGERS-FREIRE FOR SOCIAL JUSTICE.

117

Ignatius could have had; or as the one conceived in the constitution of the Society of Jesus. In this sense, the ACU is a 'mini-Society.' MI, our group, would not be a 'mini-Society' in so far as the legislative or executive structure is concerned, but rather in its characteristic depth, its spiritual background and sharing of life.

Theme 4: The Wives of the Former Jesuits

The presence of the spouses in the group was one of the main themes brought about by the founding members in their depictions of the creation and development of the MI, including the exercise of MI's proper leadership style. They leave no doubt that the issue had pros and cons. Let MI-7 start with a description of his recollections:

> The presence of the wives, which was something that I had not previously experienced - in my Marian congregation, during my college years, or while in the Society of Jesus with their characteristics, their sensibilities, their very special vision, in my experience, though it was something somewhat restricting in some way lent a very pleasant and familiar tone, witty, joyful, that certainly helped the matrimonial life and exerted certain richness in the intramarital world. But at the same time our special and peculiar way of seeing and perceiving things, with its unusual peculiarities and masculine style was judged with little possibilities of achieving completion the moment our wives were brought into the scene.

There are other opinions that deal with the problem in a much less lenient and sensitive way. MI-2 starts his analysis bluntly: "The Institute takes – in my opinion – an erroneous turn when its desire to increase the number, as well as other reasons, leads them to accept the

wives of the individuals who formed the group." MI-2 goes back to
the difficulties involved in forming a group with the characteristics of
Magister: "The tension produced by an institution that already comes
with rules, with specific objectives, with certain expectations, are almost
similar to entering the Seminary." MI-2 claims that he always told
the leadership of Magister not to include the spouses without going
through the proper selection channels like every other member added
to the founding group. MI-2 insists on making his point clear: "Since
an interview did not take place to accept the members with a defined
and clear criteria, and entry to the institute was granted simply for being
the wife of one of the original members, with rights equal to others,
given the actual situation of the culture we live in, it was a dangerous
decision." MI-2 sees many problems with the inclusion of this *ipso
facto*-group of spouses: "The wives do not have anything in common
regarding the formation and the years in which they grew up; the only
ties they share in common is that they are all wives of ex-Jesuits, and are
women who, in many instances – in as much as I was able to observe -
are very strong."

For MI-2 the spouse group actually had different objectives in mind:
"And, obviously, the objectives that the ex-Jesuits had of becoming
united were not the same as those of the women." The former Jesuits
went through a lot of experiences and accepted many insights about
living and service styles: "The women had not joined a novitiate or
seminary, the women had not made vows, the women had not made a
commitment of this nature, they did not have a high spirit of generosity
standard, nor of service, they had not gone through these transforming
processes, they did not know what it was to spend eight, ten, twenty years
in a first-class institution such as a seminary or a Jesuitical scholastic
institution. No wonder, the Jesuits have been called the Marines of the
Catholic Church." The presence of the spouses in the group creates
several new issues in the middle of the group:

> There is another problem, and it is that the husband,
> the ex-Jesuit, has to present himself to the group not as
> an individual, as it would have been without the wives,

MAGISTER: THE PHENOMENON OF MISSION AND
CAMARADERIE ROGERS-FREIRE FOR SOCIAL JUSTICE.

119

but as a couple. His wife is present, therefore all the tensions of the marriage are brought into the group, and the personality of the individual who is present with his wife is somewhat obscured, since he has to be careful about what he says, give her the opportunity to speak, and recognize that she has a different point of view. Finally, a dynamics is established among the women. The women start to become competitive with one another, and those issues are brought to the Magister Institute, greatly overshadowing the former dynamics of the organization.

MI-2 compares the natural camaraderie experienced among former Jesuits with the new situation and states: "this relationship among the former Jesuits is difficult to understand by our wives and they don't have the necessary elements in their life experiences to even approach this union, this closeness experienced among their husbands the former Jesuits." For MI-2 the group went through a lot of pain consolidating and finally attaining all those beautiful characteristics of camaraderie they have already expressed. Jesuits and former Jesuits are strong personalities, according to MI-2: "It is obvious that the personality of each ex-Jesuit was very clearly well defined; the former Jesuits were people who, up to a certain point, failed in their vocation, for one reason or another, and who have had the opportunity of straightening their lives in another professional career and who have been very successful in those careers. And being already older individuals, it would have been very difficult for this group to develop and mature, even without the presence of the wives." When coming to evaluate the degree of difficulty the Magister Institute went through, after considering the presence in the group of other couples who never had any experience with the Jesuits nor any substantive level of formation comparable to the former Jesuits, MI-1 has the following to mention: "It seems to me that all this made it difficult to avoid frictions, jealousies, questions about those who exerted some type of authority. Those who joined at a later time started to question the extension of this authority and how far was the authority of those who were later added to the group, men as well as women." According to the majority of former Jesuits (MI-1, MI-2, MI-3, MI-4, MI-5, MI-6 and MI-7) the presence of the subgroup with a different agenda and purpose facilitated a time of misunderstanding and the final separation of the Magister Institute in two, mostly a division following differences in formation, experiences, purpose, and kind of mutual commitment. MI-6 sees the changes taking place in the life of the group and notices the changes from the original purpose. When he speaks he is describing the functioning of the group as one entire unity after the former Jesuits accepted their wives and several couples without experience of Jesuits life. At this time the group became a CLC. This moment is the one MI-6 describes so well: "Even the idea of having an Institute faded out, it went to a secondary place of importance because what it became of the group was a prayer group, that is to say, a Christian Life Community. And, sure enough, this was to me a turnaround of 180 degrees. This modified all the psychological elements that intervene in the development of a *sui generis* group affecting its principal variables such like goals, leadership, and internal-external communication."

MI-4 summarizes this stage the following way: "It seems that the addition of the spouses and the non-Jesuit-related couples made it difficult for the original purpose and living style to continue, including the typical Magister's leadership style. When the two representatives from each group agreed to separate, and the group was effectively divided, delicacy and gentleness in our communications prevailed making it possible to reach this moment of common dialogue and understanding. It remains, after all have been done and said, to design a new strategy to deal with these complex realities. The approach taken by Magister's membership is to tackle one issue at the time with no *apuro* (hurry) and no preconditions."

Theme 5: Collaboration with the Jesuits

"Collaboration with the Jesuits has been a hot topic since the foundation of the Magister Institute" says MI-4 in an effort to focus this discussion. "Originally former Jesuits were kind of reticent and distant, though no one would deny that deep down inside of us we all wished collaboration to be possible and viable, yet we never suspected that back then in time, the conditions of possibility were not present in the Jesuit Community of Miami," remembers MI-4 in his depiction of the creation and development of Magister. MI-4 makes the point clearly and loudly: "During these five years there were some individual Jesuits who approached us in a very nice and affable way; yet, I think we all agree that as a community or organization the Jesuits have not given us any invitation or answer," says MI-4. The different founding members coincide in recognizing several individual Jesuits as very friendly and interested in talking with them. MI-3 describes his recollections of those first days of Magister, showing some kind of ambivalence:

I believe that our own memories, our own previous experiences were impacting how much desire we had or not to participate in the Society of Jesus. Initially, I would say that there was quite a strong effort of not having anything to do formally with the Jesuits. There was a position of approach-distance, but interrelated with a desire of collaboration and affiliation, which I believe were opposing feelings. With the few Jesuits of the community of Miami which whom I either spoke or heard speak about this subject, they amply expressed to us positive comments at the individual level. It was as if they did not want to be in a compromising position before the other members of the Jesuit community in Miami, to say, 'We are getting together with a group of ex-Jesuits who have this positive attitude.' They thought it was wonderful that we were involved in this venture of reuniting ex-Jesuits.

MI-6 confirms the Jesuit strategy used with the group: "I talked to a few Jesuits in the Miami community, and, at the personal level, they would show me acceptance and positive feelings. But, when in public, they would say nothing. It was like if they would not want to commit themselves in front of the other Jesuits." MI-6 continues with his understanding of the specific encounters had with the current Jesuits: "Individually, they seemed to say that the idea of creating a group of Ex-Jesuits with the potential for a dialog was wonderful. In other words, they had the impression that the group not only was expressing respect and admiration for the Society of Jesus, but it showed the same love and enthusiasm for the things of St, Ignatius."

MI-6 makes his point a little more clearly: "We would find them very agreeable, as I said before, at the confidential level, individually, but not at a collective or community level. They would not even say a word about it in front of third parties. They would not have wanted to give the impression that they had a favorable impression about the group. I never heard from them any comment insinuating that this was a bad idea; on the contrary, they would find what we were attempting to accomplish a formidable idea."

As explained by MI-3, MI-4, and MI-6 the former Jesuits had an original negativity or lack of expectations towards collaboration with the Jesuits. Almost simultaneously and following these initial founding moments former Jesuits expected this collaboration or dialogue about possible collaboration to take place almost as a sign of the first gesture of their friendship. Now evidence contradicting these expectations and collaboration objectives will be presented here. In a brusque tone and antagonizing most former Jesuits' expectations MI-1 states:

> From the beginning you wanted to include the Jesuits in this matter. As for me, I always defended the position that whatever you desired to do it should be done independently   from us, from the Jesuits; so that you would not be influenced, so that you would not see us from point 'X' or 'Y'; and so that you may do whatever you freely would decide and desire to do independently from us. I openly decided not to engage in a helping relationship with you, quite consciously, with the thought in mind that your personal and group development was your personal and group business and I and the other Jesuits should not influence you in making decisions one way or another; ultimately because we as Jesuits owe you respect for your independence and maturity.

MI-1 makes the point of allowing the former Jesuits do their thing in an independent way, and make sure the Jesuits allowed them from their own free will and at their own pace to reach some consensus and cohesion as a group. MI-4 takes on MI-1 and goes further with the argument: "Yes, I think we made a mistake by emphasizing too much, and too soon collaboration with the Jesuits. We should have developed by ourselves in freedom, and only then, try to approach the Jesuits and have conversations leading to individual or group collaboration. The fact that we did not see at one time beyond becoming a CLC member community, or the fact that those of us who did not feel satisfied with the CLC model of organization and life style did not stand up and argued our way in the group, meant for the MI that we continued to dream about Jesuit collaboration perhaps with some sort of emotional dependence on the Jesuits." For MI-1 the independence and maturity of the group meant above everything else that the members could hear themselves respectfully calling and summoning each other: "That you may reunite with your past and your present. It seems to me that this is important, especially after many years, after you have made personal contact and – in some way – have felt summoned and called by one another."

MI-4 brings to the discussion the conversations and dialogues he sustained with the other members of the Magister: "After providing to MI-2 and MI-6 the ideas proposed by MI-I about collaboration with the Jesuits, and after bringing forward the emphatic rejection of becoming a CLC community, they both agreed that Jesuit collaboration was overemphasized, and was a mistake to continue with it as a major goal of the group. MI-7 was very clear in accepting collaboration was a mistake of the group, and emphasized our independent way of becoming MI as the ideal way of proceeding." MI-1 continues with the idea of Magister's independent way toward maturity and cohesion as a group: "I believe the responsibility is yours, since we should not be an obstacle to your development and I believe that you, as a group, should mature, come to an agreement, reach conclusions, and see the possibilities of working together in a way that we would not inappropriately influence you at all." MI-1 sees maturity first, cohesion second, and then all sorts of collaborative attempts: "Then, I believe that is, to a certain point, advantageous to you and to us. I believe that you could, in some way, work with us, I do not see it as impossible; but one thing is the group and another individuals, and those concepts should be respected."

After five years of group activity, the members of Magister should be ready for what MI-1 has observed and seen, to engage individually and as a group in a formal collaboration with the Jesuits:

> I believe that now you have reached a higher level of maturity because you have risen to a new echelon of conscience of what you have lived and have been doing on your own. Then, I see this as something that, in a way, had to take place despite the first ideal or goal that you placed on the table about collaboration with the Jesuits and which seemed quite good to me, and that I supported and blessed, but your personal and group circumstances had to mature.

For MI-1 this maturity process that has taken place these past five years completed the process:

> It was necessary to allow you to truly mature in that type of experience and - before making any decision of joining the Christian Life Community, or the ACU, or a group 'X' called Magister – you had to reach a level of maturity in the personal experience of the group with its past, its present and its future. This process of maturity and this type of analysis would help you see the lights and shadows of the Magister Institute as it should be.

Now MI-1 feels the group might be ready to formally get into a collaboration process with the Jesuits. MI-1 insists that each member should be respected and group actions should only take place when cohesion and maturity allow the group to reach consensus in these important issues: "What's more, I would say that as a group we are going

MAGISTER: THE PHENOMENON OF MISSION AND
CAMARADERIE ROGERS-FREIRE FOR SOCIAL JUSTICE.

125

to collaborate with the Society of Jesus, but each one is going to offer his services for the work of his choice, for whatever initiative of his own choosing, respecting the vocation of each member, and – at the same time – the needs to which they are called. If it is convenient for me, I will go; if it is not convenient for me, I will not go. I wish to contribute but I do not like this, I would like something else. That is, that you will feel free to cooperate." MI-1 finishes this section of his depiction knowingly directing a message to the former Jesuits: "Are we capable of working together? Are we capable of getting organized in the future or do we need to mature? What do we need to mature as a Magister group? Are we capable to, again, sit down and dialogue and find out what God requires of us, how can we serve, which have been our difficulties, and how have we overcome them?" Thinking that Magister has gone through a lot of conflict and difficulties, MI-1 challenges those of the group that might not feel the calls and summons of the rest of the group: "Or have the difficulties divided us, have they separated us, have they been an obstacle to becoming more systematic, more organic, and able to be identified as a group?"

This section on collaboration with the Jesuits seems to have been interpreted by MI-1 and MI-5 as a summons and a call: "To understand the possible future incorporation of some of the work performed by the Jesuits today, it is necessary to understand that the Jesuits in this part of the world, concretely in Miami, perform three types of work." MI-5 speaks very highly of the efforts already shown by the former Jesuits and starts to provide concrete evidence of this collaboration: "Well, yes, I think that the group has contributed in many ways. For example, the collaboration that was done in Casa Manresa, with talks about psychology, with help in the spiritual retreats, etc., that I have heard has taken place; the type of collaboration, including financial help, donations, etc., to some Jesuit institutions, I think this is truly collaborating work." MI-5 goes now to a generalization of the entire group and of the entire possibilities of collaboration: "As for me, the interesting part is not so much that the individual member of the Magister group is working or collaborating in a concrete work with a specific position. Rather, it is the fact that they have come closer, be it as a group, and that if, the Society of Jesus would extend its hand and ask for collaboration, the Magister group would be willing to provide it." MI-5 then takes a look at five years of collaboration efforts and concludes: "Moreover, it seems to me that comparing the time previous to the foundation of the group, with what you have already achieved, it can be concluded that there has been progress." MI-5 then looks at the group and sees it this way: "And I tell you, the group is still a work in progress, it is not a completed work. While we are living, we are walking, and in that sense I think that there could be more collaboration in the future than there has been until now; but there has been some already now. This collaboration has been incipient, yes, but visible and recognizable by all."

Theme 6: The Leadership Style of Magister

Former Jesuits were ten professionals, experts in different fields of knowledge. MI-2 remembers that: "They are well prepared and each one of them believes he is an expert in theology, in philosophy, in sociology, etc." This information was provided to highlight the degree of difficulty involved in the coordination of Magister Institute. Non-directiveness was the strategy to match this degree of difficulty. MI-3 remembers key details of these moments: "It seems to me that the leadership was paramount in the formation of all that. It was like an invitation. It seems that the one who would later be the coordinator, in fact you, played a very important role regarding a convocation of old friends who had shared all that experience of the Society of Jesus, and got together to drink coffee, and to see if we wanted to do something together, without any specific agenda, merely to share and explore options."

The only possible way out for the group was each one freely finding the next move. MI-6 provides a very comprehensive depiction of the leadership style of Magister's Executive Committee: "I am the kind of psychologist who likes inclusion, who likes facilitation. To me, actually, these are the words that better describe this leadership period.

MAGISTER: THE PHENOMENON OF MISSION AND
CAMARADERIE ROGERS-FREIRE FOR SOCIAL JUSTICE.

127

In addition, leadership style meant this thing of allowing people to feel good about what they were saying, no matter what they were saying."

This observation has to do with the creation of the atmosphere for understanding and acceptance to be experienced, for freedom to be exercised by each one: "On the part of the group in general, and I saw also this from the very beginning, it was not important what any group member would say. I found in these meetings a significant level of maturity. We have to highlight the observation of the fact that the members were seasoned men. There was a definite respect for the other person's opinion. I never witnessed endless discussions or personal insults. None of these things ever happened."

These characteristics described by MI-6, one of the psychologists in the group, brought to the open the atmosphere of permissiveness and the experience of freedom which facilitated the most intimate expressions. Again MI-6 states: "Consequently, those who were decided continued on in spite of the fact that at the time the vision might not be very clear to anyone – the goals and objectives took a long time to become obvious. This whole process took form with time, interactions, and many meetings. Then, after a certain period of time it became more evident what to do."

The non-directive, person-centered strategy of the EC was being effective in awakening the most creative expressions. MI-6 continues: "In addition, there was another aspect that facilitated the process of the group. The level of participation in the group was very high. In other words, there was a partaking in the leadership process. We would ask many questions, we would consult many issues. However, these elements disappeared when the CLC factor came to be a predominant element. The core group (the Ex-Jesuits) could continue to understand each other very easily and I think this helped the whole process of group dynamics."

The description of the leadership style of the EC of Magister is being completed little by little. MI-6 states: "A very interesting thing that I could perceive was that, from the point of view of leadership, you came to play a key role. You handled the process with sensitivity, love, and the ability to facilitate dialog. The more the group would meet, the more these qualities of yours were evident. I, personally, liked very much and I felt very comfortable with your non-directive leadership style that slowly became the central component of the Magister style of leadership."

The leadership basic elements MI-6 has described are nonthreatening environment, person-centeredness, non-directiveness, mutual respect, mutual understanding, mutual acceptance, and a generalized facilitating attitude. MI-6 also describes the team effort carried by the EC providing a generalized facilitating environment: "In this very same direction, I also saw other members in a non-directive and facilitating attitude trying to unite the group and not to divide it, helping the group members to feel at ease and avoiding the position of exclusion insisting more in the inclusion of everyone in the group."

MI-7 describes this atmosphere as created by key members of Magister's EC:

> The periodic meetings started with that general attitude, and I must express that - little by little - it began to reappear, a vision started to form, a humble desire to place the talents of that small group - which at the time was formed by four or five - to function, so that this communion of visions could produce some fruit, in the society we lived. The reunions turned out to be pleasant, there was a congenial dimension, happy, communitarian, affective, and the directors, coordinators – the three 'heads', to say so – and the coordinator carried the reunions effortlessly, with ample freedom for everything, helping us -who were there - to feel much at ease.

These descriptions complete the MI-6's depiction of the leadership style of the Magister Institute: "Regarding the direction of the group, truly the tactfulness and the quality of the care taken, even during the times of tension, at the end, it was something extraordinary. In other words, I do not think that any one was left with a bad after-taste. I believe that this is something that could still be experimented in the future, specifically in terms of members of orders or religious congregations that could opt for something of this kind. I believe that this is something perfectly possible, which needs to be done with much tact, and perhaps the experiences of this small group could help to bring it to fruition in the most adequate manner." MI-7 describes the leadership style of Magister by providing descriptions of the members of Magister that influenced the most in the creation of the team of equals' spirit and leadership style: "There are several important points specifically regarding the cohesion of the masculine group, who where the – let us call them – bonding members, because they were present, there, through their experience in the Society of Jesus. And these are the characteristics: First, an affinity of the affective type, congeniality, a very special camaraderie, and an ability to treat one another with ease. Second, a vision, an intellect; in the fundamental factors, very much in common, there was a grand scale participation of intellectual understanding, which – logically – helped a great deal." The understanding and the acceptance was very unique, according to MI-7. He continues this narration and describes efforts provided by small steering committees within the entire group dynamics: "But there was a community of thought and feeling, and that, after all -even though at the beginning the members of Magister did not have an explicit direction or leadership – or, let us say, not everyone had a job inside the institution, there were many leaders there, in other words, they were people accustomed to assume responsibility."

MI-3 looks at this group and sees logic in the leadership style: this is a community of leaders. MI-3 states: "It was almost a community of leaders, I would say, very capable individuals; the list was impressive, when we began to make up the roles and so, to see the credentials that formed that community." MI-7 feels the value of these communications and goes into the managerial responsibilities: "Logically, we continue to show our gratitude to the coordinator, who is the one who has facilitated that these internal feelings and this vision may be exteriorized in the manner we are doing now." In another summary MI-7 finds the EC as the ultimate unit of leadership: "Had it not been, nonetheless, in the case of some of us – myself included - for the orientation, enthusiasm, and drive of the original group, of the three who started this thing, this would have not existed, it would have not taken place."

Summary of the Findings (Themes)

This study tells the story of the creation, foundation, and leadership style of Magister Institute. A group of ten former Jesuits gathered on April of 2004 and tried to stay together with the original intention of doing some apostolic work in common. The group related well and enjoyed each other's company. They named a steering committee in charge of delineating the main guidelines of the group and leading them into a more structured organization. Because they all had a common background of Jesuit education and style of life, based on the Spiritual Exercises and the Jesuit scholastic formation program, the steering committee drafted a graphic and written blueprint of the future bylaws of the group, including its name, Magister Institute. The discovery of the Christian Life Communities led the incipient group to seriously consider becoming part of them. Once the steering committee could guarantee the independence of the group from the Jesuits, the group did not see any reason prohibiting joining these CLC organizations. In an effort to join the lay movement within the Catholic Church and avoid the negative designation of ex-Jesuits or former Jesuits, the group accepted the proposal to allow their wives to join the group as full members. Once the group was open to females, other couples were accepted, though most of them lacked the necessary background to rank as equals in formation and world vision to the former Jesuits. After some time, a bit over six months since the group accepted new members, the reality of the internal differences started to show itself in discrepancies and misunderstandings. The fact that all of the non-Jesuit couple newcomers were intimate friends of one of the EC's founding members, contributed to raising within the main original group a subgroup with a different purpose and style of life from those of the founding members and former Jesuits. The reality of bitter discussions, different concepts of mission, concept of apostolate-oriented group

MAGISTER: THE PHENOMENON OF MISSION AND
CAMARADERIE ROGERS-FREIRE FOR SOCIAL JUSTICE.

131

versus prayer and socialization oriented subgroup, brought about the necessity of seriously discussing the division of the two groups into two separate organizations, one remaining with a majority of founding members as Magister Institute, and the other acquiring a new name and a different conception of group life and activities. Now, through these individual phenomenological depictions, six themes have become paramount in their review and evaluation of these five years of common or separate group life. The main themes were, first, the high levels of camaraderie among the former Jesuits. The second theme was the attraction/mistrust the Jesuits elicited from the former Jesuits. Thirdly, the CLC was conceived by the majority as a mistaken step in the direction of finding group identity. Fourthly, asking former Jesuits' wives to join them as members of Magister Institute was seen by the majority as another mistake. Fifthly, the goal of Jesuit collaboration from the start was also a problematic move. Finally, the leadership style of the former Jesuit's EC was non-directive and reached high levels of acceptance among former Jesuits. The group is "under construction" as it were and may still develop and mature making the collaboration with the Jesuits a reachable goal.

Chapter Summary

This chapter started with an introduction of the entire study. It was followed by highlighting the personal characteristics of the group being used as a sample. The interviews were analyzed in themes and ultimately six major themes were developed and accepted. The characteristics of camaraderie were described by the group of founding members. The intertwining of the concepts of attraction and mistrust has kept collaboration dreams at a distance. The CLC transformation of the Magister Institute was questioned by the majority of former Jesuit members. The automatic inclusion of the wives in group was viewed by the majority of those interviewed as a mistake. The initial goal of collaboration with the Jesuits was also challenged and the necessity of group maturity and common understanding was emphasized. Finally, a very positive and highly regarded style of leadership was used by the members of the Executive Committee creating an atmosphere of freedom, mutual acceptance and respect. Finally, a narration of the story of the five years of the group was offered extracted from the quotations from each one of the research participants.

CHAPTER V

DISCUSSION OF THE FINDINGS

Introduction

This study examined the leadership styles and other significant lived experiences connected with the foundation of the Magister Institute. Most of the members of the original group of ten ex-Jesuits experienced various transitional stages.

The Magister Institute is an official member of the Christian Life Community, the largest worldwide lay group associated with the Society of Jesus (S.J.). This Institute was initiated in 2004 in Miami-Dade County by ten former Jesuits of the Antilles Province of the Society of Jesus who first gathered socially at the invitation of one of the former Jesuits and priests to discuss the possibility of engaging a common apostolic work. In time, this unstructured group of former Jesuits, assisted by appropriate leadership strategies, moved from being distant and separate from the Jesuits to aspiring to become collaborators of the Society of Jesus. The minutes, reflections, and assembled materials of the Magister Institute's collected papers from 2004-2009 highlight important moments of the progress of these former Jesuits as they developed into a vibrant group affiliated with the Christian Life Communities. The study explored the leadership processes that guided these men in their sincere search for their roots, identity, and a reoriented mission in life.

This study was a qualitative investigation of the impact the Executive Committee's leadership style and other group processes had on the creation and development of the Magister Institute. It is hoped that, at a time when increasing numbers leave their religious organizations within the Catholic Church, this study can be helpful to religious organizations who seek to understand the journey of members who leave. This study may also show how, with appropriate leadership, former members can provide services to religious organizations, parishes, and communities and help reduce the workload on overburdened religious and priestly personnel (Magister Institute Collected Papers, 2004-2008; McDonough & Bianchi, 2002).

Summary of the Study

Purpose

This study was a phenomenological study, based mostly on individual interviews and dialogues attempting to describe and explore the leadership styles of these individuals and their feelings, emotions, and ideas leading to the creation, and establishment, of the Magister Institute. The objective was to analyze and synthesize the individual depictions of the inception of the group in its process of becoming the Magister Institute through the time of its split into two distinct organizations. These descriptions have been integrated in order to formulate a composite, comprehensive depiction.

This study offers key guidelines and interpretation of the processes these men experienced. Thousands of similar men and women, and numerous dioceses and religious congregations around the world could benefit from this research.

A final reason justifying this study is the lack of serious and trustworthy literature on Latin American former Jesuits (Saez, S.J., personal communication, 2009). As far as the researcher could ascertain, there is nothing in the literature about any former Jesuits gathering themselves into a group that has accepted as an aspiration to work with the Jesuits as collaborators. This study is the first of its kind and hopefully will encourage other researchers to continue in a similar fashion and enhance the understanding of the leadership styles' description

Significance

This investigation was vital because it studied an unprecedented event in the history of the Catholic Church, namely, the tentative reacceptance of ten former Jesuits including five priests as a group they called the Magister Institute.

The study described and analyzed the group members' perceptions of processes of culture sharing and leadership style through interviews, journals, letters, and other personal documents as they strove to reestablish their roots, identity, and mission in life. A culture-sharing phenomenological-heuristic study of this group of former Jesuits in their quest for personal and group identity and mission in life elicited new insight into religious/ethnic processes involved in similar separation-reassociation research studies and the successful leadership styles that guided them.

Within the Catholic Church, priests and religious who have separated themselves from their ministries or official religious organizations have traditionally remained distant from their former religious communities (McDonough & Bianchi, 2002). Today, nevertheless, there seems to be a growing tendency towards more understanding. Some recent related cases could be considered a slight indication of new trends pointing in the direction of a long-range true reconciliation (Magister Institute collected papers, 2004-2009).

The case of these former Jesuits is thought provoking. It includes a positive trend towards a future enriching re-association with a traditional religious institution and a break with its historic rigidity. This statement has been qualified and clarified by the facts surfaced by the phenomenological analysis of interviews, letters, notes, and other relevant material collected in this research. This study has offered new insight into the leadership style and phenomenological processes involved in the life transitions of these men.

In fact, not all of the former Jesuits may consider their collaboration with the current members of the Society of Jesus an act of true reconciliation. At first glance, the true perception of the group of former Jesuits did not appear to be evident with the scarce information gathered in the collected papers of the Magister Institute. Clarification of these components, relationships, and their meaning was obtained as one of the main goals of the research.

This study focused on the narrative descriptions—interviews (approximately an hour each) and conversations (of up to twenty minutes)—of the lived experiences of each participant-observer chosen to be part of the sample. Their comprehensive descriptions have been further elucidated through the help of documents, letters, notes, and any other personal records. The study has focused solely on the description of the life experiences, narrated in a live and phenomenologically accurate way by the members of the research sample. Every effort was made to exclude any foreign interpretation to the co-researchers' individual vivid comprehensive narrations and their resulting depictions (Moustakas, 1994). These depictions involved phenomenological processes of a journey of re-association and reconciliation. The conduct of this study required a very open and acceptant attitude on the part of the researcher, allowing the co-researchers to express their feelings and emotions about the creation of the Magister Institute, the sensitive stories of their breakaway from the Jesuits, and in some cases, their second breakaway, this time between those who remained in the original Magister Institute and those who created a new Christian Life Community.

The interviews and other exchanges of information between the main researcher and the participants focused on the depictions obtained from each of the research participants.

Method

The outcome of this study was a composite depiction of the development Magister Institute as it evolved from an initial informal group of ten former Jesuits to a formal foundation y six former Jesuits, its development, maturation, and ultimately separation into two groups. The final individual depiction of events, personal implications, perceptions, and life experiences were gathered, analyzed and synthesized. The researcher developed the overall synthesis and depiction, thus providing clarifying explanations and understanding of the creation and establishment of this Institute.

The research methods and strategies were founded on the qualitative tradition of inquiry as they are interpreted and refined by the phenomenological heuristic research model. A six-step process followed the completion of the collection of the data. The six steps are as follows:

Initial engagement,

Immersion into the topic and question,

Incubation,

Illumination,

Explication, and

Creative synthesis.

All of these steps are interconnected by means of dialogue. Basically, the researcher actively promoted the other participants to rethink and make new judgments of the phenomenon under scrutiny after other points of view were accumulated and new syntheses re-drafted. As it is elucidated by Moustakas (1994), this interaction yielded layers of depth and meaning, ultimately providing more in-depth and accurate depictions of the foundation of the Magister Institute.

This feedback to the research participants brought to the study the necessary process of verification and rendered the understanding and consequent narrative of the phenomenon more accurate and reflective of reality as perceived by each of the participants.

The researcher's expectation of more similitude at the end among the individual narratives demonstrated greater accuracy in depicting the creation of the Magister Institute. This special effort of comparing and sharing the opinions of the founding members, a true process of triangulation and member checking, functioned as a guarantee of the rigor and trustworthiness of the study (Moustakas, 1994). Yet, the final synthesis has been the responsibility of the researcher as he combined all different narratives and expressed them in their uniqueness and in their commonalities.

This was a heuristic study which had several features involving psychological phenomenology. Here are some unique characteristics of this heuristic approach on which this study has been based. First, while other approaches emphasize a certain distance from the phenomenon, this heuristic study used ongoing relationships and communication with the phenomenon under consideration. In addition, this heuristic research achieved a true depiction of the personal meaning and significance of the phenomenon.

Heuristic methodology led to an act of synthesis, which in itself was also an act of creative discovery. As in heuristic studies, communication increased after the main depictions were handed in and further information from the depictions of other participants provided a basis for new dialogues. This heuristic research concentrated on the recreation of the lived experience from the frame of reference of the person who experienced it. Other narratives, documents, journals, diaries, or even dialogues have completed and confirmed the depiction, and have not been used to change their embedded meaning. The researcher arrived at the final synthesis after following the six prescribed steps, guaranteeing purity and trustworthiness of the qualitative approach selected and recommended for this study.

The researcher was nondirective and permissive in the dialogues and interviews, respecting the uniqueness of each depiction and dialogue, and simultaneously, as Guba and Lincoln (1981) recommend, developing a global sense of the phenomenon. The immersion and incubation into the phenomenon leading to the illumination, the insight, and the synthesis that pooled everything together were necessary steps required of the researcher in utilizing the instrument of this research (Moustakas, 1990, 1994).

Limitations

Phenomenological-heuristic research required a constant engagement of the researcher in the central phenomenon and with the research participants (Moustakas, 1994). The researcher, in his incessant dialogue with all participant-observers, increased his knowledge of the phenomenon under investigation, and simultaneously experienced creative self-discovery. This subjective involvement of the researcher made his experience rich and unique and gave him a very special vantage point from which to describe and communicate his allocated depictions (Moustakas, 1994). In all six themes, the researcher was led to reconsider points of view and the addition of new ideas.

The relationship between the researcher and the participants was one of closeness and mutual reciprocity. Only the researcher performed the collection of data, codification, and theme finding. This could have had the implication of bias and possible lack of objectivity. However, the post-interview dialogues made him one more witness offering a different and not necessarily partial viewpoint and depiction. The research became more credible, that is to say, it brought out more truth to the descriptions of the phenomenon from one extra participant-observer receptive to new and antagonizing perspectives. Although very personal and even passionate, it completed a multi-faceted description of the phenomenon, thus, ascertaining the non-biased character of the researcher's point of view. The level of reflexivity of the researcher, accepting the possibility of his own personal bias, helped to make his professional participation trustworthy. This trustworthiness was increased by the researcher's showing knowledge and expertise in the non-directive and person-centered approach.

A second limitation of this study rested on the ability and willingness of the group members to provide truthful and voluntary information in the interviews. The depiction of each interview itself was tested by comparing it with other members' interview descriptions, that is, by triangulating it. The use of documents and dialogues has served as another instance of multiple data source, and this became a core triangulation process with focus on the interviews.

These limitations and possible biases were part of the reality of weaknesses faced and dealt with in this investigation. Through a process of reflexivity (Milinki, 1999), these instances of limitation were turned into assets and key evolving processes, making this study's credibility and trustworthiness, the pillars of the validity structure, acceptable and scientifically plausible (Lincoln & Guba, 1985; Patton, 2002).

Discussion of the Findings (Themes)

Discussion

This study consisted in non-structured and open-ended interviews of five former Jesuits, founding members of Magister Institute, and two current Jesuits of the area of Miami-Dade County, Florida. The study followed the qualitative method and was based on the phenomenological tradition of inquiry with the orientation and interpretation given to it by the heuristic method as understood by Clark Moustakas. The study was also inscribed within the tradition of non-directive and person-centered approach of Carl Rogers and the critical pedagogy of Paulo Freire. The interviews were non-structured and followed the main questions as provided in the study and cited in Appendix D of this dissertation. The research participants described very freely and openly their perception of the creation, development, and leadership style of Magister Institute. Their descriptions were very rich and creative, each one of them providing new ideas and provocative reflections never expected by the researcher. They did not speak with each other about their expositions before they were interviewed, as they verbally expressed to the researcher. This was considered by the researcher as most curious and challenging when analyzing the transcripts and discovering the different themes with the intention of describing the true story of the creation, development, and leadership strategies of the Magister Institute. The story has resulted in one not-so-simple version of the facts, and in a multi-dimensional analysis of the same facts experienced by the entire group of five founding members.

Let it be said, first, that the six themes running across the transcripts of the majority of the seven research participants were very creative and made the interpretations of the experiences of the group seem reasonable, coherent, and congruent with the entire sum of the depictions made by the interviewees. The majority of the members tackled the key elements of the phenomenon to be explained and offered truly remarkable reasoned explanations (See the graphic interpretation of the themes according to research participants in Appendix F). Each participant emphasized one or two themes; actually, themes were selected as such by the researcher because of the number of times concepts and ideas, connected with core meaning of the themes selected were expressed by a participant. Once ideas were grouped into themes and themes were found to be overextended through the entire gamut of the participants, the issue that remained came down to selecting the most representative and meaningful themes of the many expressed by the corresponding author. A word becomes relevant and is considered to be a part of a theme when it has been repeated several times in different paragraphs. A word also becomes significant when the same word is repeated many times in one paragraph. A word can be considered to be a part of the theme also according to the profundity or uniqueness of the expression of the theme. Several words can become a theme when this theme may help clarify a point. The way authority was interpreted and exercised by one member of Magister was not included in the findings because the topic of the dissertation was leadership as exercised by the Executive Committee of Magister Institute. To accept the challenge expressed by one member would have derailed the focus of the dissertation into endless though spicy and at times no doubt brilliant discussions among the participants. A researcher's job, as the policeman's lot of Shakespeare, "is not a happy one."

Secondly, there were some points difficult to integrate into the common vision offered by the group of seven. Those points were mentioned, though their interpretation when the other points of view had been described might have helped clear apparent contradictions when originally expressed by the research participant. The issue of the experience of the wives, and the assimilation of the CLC philosophy and way of life became understandable only when the themes were dealt with so extensively by several of the founding members or current Jesuits. The power of the themes to clarify old issues became evident, and the researcher decided not to summarize them again in a special section of Chapter IV.

Thirdly, the leadership style of the Executive Committee was very clear at the end of the chapter after each theme was described making it redundant to engage again in a distinct and rich final description. The non-directive, respectful, delicate and sensitive way founding members were treated from the beginning and treated each other always became evident after all members depicted their leadership in similar descriptive ways. The founding members group, the focus of this dissertation and heart of the phenomenon to be studied, had a style of leadership among themselves that well deserved the description of "team of equals" and "management by consensus." The entire group of research participants coincided in judging their own style of leadership as paramount and ideal. The only discrepancy with this finding of the study occurs when the leadership style of the entire group is considered. As it was noted several times by MI-2, MI-4, MI-6 and MI-7 the style of leadership had to change when the group had also suffered profound transformation. These groups were two: one, the founding group of former Jesuits, and the focus of this study; and the other a bigger, expanded group made up by their wives and the addition of three couples and one individual woman as described by MI-3, MI-2, MI-1, MI-6 and MI-4.

The fact that some members do not mention one theme or another should not be interpreted as holding a negative position on the issue, as MI-2 and MI-7 expressed in post-interview dialogues. Since the topic was the core group, as described by MI-6, this issue of the leadership style of the bigger group of former Jesuits, their wives, and several other couples with no former connection with the Jesuit way of life, had to be left without extended treatment in this study. The researcher, however, to maintain his internal congruence and outward transparency did not continue his advancement into new steps of the study until he gave detailed answer to these unexpected apparent contradictions to the focus of the study. This issue concretely took the researcher two days (about ten hours of work in total and ten pages long) to get it resolved in a personal satisfactory manner. This strategy is used to promote personal internal congruence and transparency which is so necessary for genuine communication. Yet, to introduce this topic into the main stream discussion of the study would, in this researcher's opinion, have taken the focus of the study in a tangential direction.

Fourthly, the methodological richness of the heuristic-phenomenological approach was evident when the researcher became the most knowledgeable person of the founding group. He was the only one directly receiving information from all research participants; and though surrounded by confidentiality, the quality and quantity of discussions and consultations allowed him to understand each person from a privileged point of view. The researcher was ready to create a synthesis with the information gathered from all the research participants. This synthesis was new even to himself.

Fifthly, the subtle change of mind taking place in the former Jesuits, through the intensive months of this study, could have never been predicted or hypothesized. The questioning of the CLC and the discovery of the simple way of becoming and developing as Magister caught many by surprise, including the researcher. The issue of collaboration with the Jesuits, an obsessing dream at the peak of its frustrating limits, evolved, matured and reprogrammed itself positively as a desire and aspiration for unity, cohesion, self-confidence, and openness to a new vocation. This new desire and emphasis has been experienced and expressed by all. The fact that all five founding members perceived a call and summons from the rest of the group to be part of the experience of Magister brought at the end a new and fresh vision of the days ahead of us. This was a way to pass over and/or disguise the sadness of the lack of response experienced from the Jesuits in the collaboration issue. The group not only passed over this negative incident but experienced an almost simultaneous sense of new peace and sweetness in the relationship with the Jesuits. How to explain these changes and these new beginnings is one issue. To recognize them is a result of the findings.

One point that needs clarification is the lack of interest of the Jesuits in the offer of the group to collaborate with them. Some former Jesuits mentioned that the level of difficulty experienced in accepting the members who abandon their institutions was similar to the one experienced in military organizations. Several members asked themselves: Is this vocation eternal and unchangeable? Some Jesuits consider religious vocation to be one. Others already accept the possibility of a second calling from God. It seems according to McDonough and Bianchi (2002) that most current Jesuits in the North American Region go through their training thinking that the former Jesuits may have received a second calling, and that they, the current Jesuits, might as well be recipient of a second calling as well. This could explain why former Jesuits in the USA might have a better chance of collaborating with the Jesuits.

Conclusions

The following conclusions are supported by the findings of this study. First, the set of characteristics described in the section A New Rogers-Freire-Goleman Paradigm of this study and attributed to the Magister Institute's leadership style were substantiated by the research participants in their interviews and post-interviews conversations and dialogues with the researcher. It should be pointed out that this MI's leadership style related only to the founding group of former Jesuits, and

MAGISTER: THE PHENOMENON OF MISSION AND
CAMARADERIE ROGERS-FREIRE FOR SOCIAL JUSTICE.

145

the study was not extended to include the complex and diverse entire 19-member group which incorporated at one time all the founding members' spouses, the new added non-Jesuit-related couples and single persons. There is one element to highlight as by-product of this detailed analysis, the perception by all the members that this was a "group or team of equals" or a "consensus management group." These two expressions seemed to convey in their minds that MI group reached the highest level of person-centeredness and attained an ideal form of personal and group consensus management.

Secondly, the short-term goal of collaboration with the Jesuits was challenged by one current Jesuit in his exposition and came out to be accepted by most of the group members once the real expectations of each were clearly exposed. This unanticipated discovery came about after a complete set of core elements of former Jesuit strivings was followed through until its furthest confines. The reasoned conception of Magister Institute included the following descriptions: "a group of equals"(MI-2, MI-3, and MI-4); "without organizational structure of any type" (MI-6, MI-3, MI-4, and MI-7); "with total flexibility"(MI-3) "our own, indigenous, home-grown, organizational framework and setting" (MI-6); and "a group endowed with efficacious solidarity to carry forward a vision of reality, in this case, Christian, Catholic, and within the Ignatian paradigm" (MI-7). Once these elements were grouped together and transformed into a vision, most of the members, starting with this researcher, accepted this new vision and emphasis as a new and more enriching goal and a substitute for the one of collaboration. The former Jesuits should have trusted in themselves and created a group based on their own personal experience. Things were supposed to be done at their own pace, under the light of their own lantern, and with their indigenous leadership style of supervision. Now the former Jesuits are able to trust in each other again and look at the Jesuits without awakening in themselves any negative feeling.

Thirdly, the method employed has shown its usefulness to study action groups in a short period of time. Once a researcher has a clear and precise idea of the methodology to be employed, and can bring to a core group of researchers persons involved in the activity in question, the use of open-ended interviews should provide the expected necessary information; of course the sample group must be selected among key persons in the life of the organization. Time and cost are two important factors to be considered when new efforts to re-orient health organizations, educational programs, and so many other service providers are urgently needed.

Fourthly, the comparison that some members made of the Magister Institute with the CLC and ACU's organizational and management styles was very enlightening and refreshing. Contradictions never explained before became understandable, and realities standing in the way were identified facilitating the pursuit of identity and mission as more viable alternatives.

Fifthly, the highlighted imbedded sense of mission of the founding members made their unity and common vision a viable alternative. MI-3 exclaimed with firmness and self-confidence: "our commitment to mission is not negotiable." This general perception of a profound and permanent bond established by former Jesuits with their sense of mission might be one of their most attractive characteristics when the values and possibilities of their collaboration are being considered.

There seems to be, also, good reason to sustain from the findings of this study that there are former Jesuits and former religious who will perceive as attractive and fulfilling collaborating with organizations and institutions of the Catholic Church.

Finally, this researcher made clear that the heuristic phenomenologic method employed to study this complex and intricate religious organization facilitated its global comprehension while shedding light to understand the uniqueness and otherness of several of its key components. This study analyzed and assessed the creation, development and leadership strategies of Magister Institute offering a global all-inclusive perspective while contributing to comprehend several core and separate elements of its standard operating style.

MAGISTER: THE PHENOMENON OF MISSION AND
CAMARADERIE ROGERS-FREIRE FOR SOCIAL JUSTICE.

147

Recommendations

Further Research

A review of the literature reveals that there is little or no research done in the Spanish world concerning former Jesuit groups' creation and/ or development. Personal communication with historians connected to Jesuit studies revealed also that little or no known literature of this type is known to exist. It seems self-evident that this study fills a gap and may act as catalytic for other similar endeavors. This study however may contribute to the knowledge of an existing reality, the former Jesuits, the former religious and the non-active priests in search of a job in the area of their training and past experience. Other studies, whether quantitative or qualitative may contribute to further understand their situation and its significance to the Church and society.

Implications

Finally, this study has a methodological and theoretical background. It is also based in the lived experience of a group of people who have been part of the phenomenon to be studied, including the main researcher. The unique experience of the study not only has provided clarification of situations and ideas, but also the betterment of the quality of leadership in concrete organizations. Hopefully this kind of dissertation contributes also by providing guidelines to replicate similar studies and thus to better organizations, groups, and communities. Studies like this reach the group and the organization with its leaders and members. It touches through the written word the minds and hearts of future students interested in advancing the cause of the groups and organizations implicated in the studies. It also provides a methodological and theoretical foundation for the scientific apparatus indispensable in producing these results. Possibly interested readers will find not only theoretical and speculative challenges in this research but also a personal invitation to receive and carry forward this humble but proud academic and scientific torch.

Chapter Summary

This chapter presented a summary of the entire theoretical and methodological foundations of this study after the heuristic phenomenological research was conducted. The purpose of this study was presented together with a summary of the significance it will have in the areas of society connected with former Jesuits, former religious, non-active priests, and religious organizations or Church services. The importance of these former religious was emphasized and the value of this study for their current religious organizations was discussed. A brief presentation of the method and its limitations was offered and its implications discussed. The findings were presented in the form of themes, the product of the analysis of the different transcribed interviews. Six themes – camaraderie, the identity of Magister, the wives, attraction and mistrust, collaboration, and leadership style – were presented and carefully interrelated by providing direct information (quotations) from each of the seven research participants. A discussion of the findings was offered and a number of conclusions was submitted. Finally, some notes were presented on the state of research after this study and the implications for practice were highlighted. Finally the researcher invited the future researcher to continue the serious and hard work by receiving and carrying forward this humble but proud academic and scientific torch.

REFERENCES

Bakan, D. (1996). Origination, self-determination, and psychology. *Journal of Humanistic Psychology, 26*(1), 9-20.

Barrett-Lennard, G. T. (1994). Toward a person-centered theory of community. *Journal of Humanistic Psychology, 34*(3), 62-86

Brink, D. C. (1987). The issue of equality and control in the client-centered approach. *Journal of Humanistic Psychology 27*(1), 27-37.

Brizuela, B., & Soler-Gallart, M. (1998). Cultural action for freedom: Editors' introduction. *Harvard Educational Review, 68*(4), 471-475.

Creswell, J. W. (1998). *Qualitative inquiry and research design.* Thousand Oaks, CA: Sage Publications.

Creswell, J. W. (2005). *Educational research.* Upper Saddle River, NJ: Pearson Prentice Hall.

Christian Life Community. (1991, January). Principios generales. Progressio, No. 36. Creswell, J. W. (1998). *Qualitative inquiry and research design.* Thousand Oaks, CA: Sage Publications.

Chrispeels, J. H., Castillo, S., & Brown, J. (2000). School leadership teams: A process model of team development. *School Effectiveness and School Improvement, II* (1), 20-27.

Cruz, J. R. (1983). *Hacia el desarrollo de la personalidad.* Santo Domingo, DR: Amigo del Hogar.

Cruz, J. R. (Collected papers 2009). *A master's degree in community psychology.* American Psychological Association, 90th Annual Convention, August 23-27, 1982, Washington, DC.

Denzin, N. K., & Lincoln, Y. S. (1998). *The landscape of qualitative research.* Thousand Oaks, CA: Sage Publications.

Drucker, P.F. (1999, March-April). Managing oneself. *Harvard Business Review.* (p. 70).

Ewen, R. B. (1998). *An introduction to theories of personality.* Mahwah, NJ: Lawrence Erlbaum Associates.

Fisher, K., & Miller, A. (1993). *Leading self-directed work teams*. New York: McGraw-Hill.

Fiske, D. W., & Shweder, R. A. (1986). *Metatheory in social science*. Chicago: University of Chicago Press.

Frankl, V. (1966). *De la Psicoterapia a la Logoterapia*. Madrid, Spain: Brevarios.

Freire, P. (1969). *La educación como práctica de la libertad*. Madrid, Spain: Siglo XXI Editores.

Freire, P. (1970). *Pedagogía del oprimido*. Madrid, Spain: Siglo Veintiuno Editores.

Freire, P. (1970). *Pedagogy of the oppressed*. New York: Seabury Press.

Goizueta, R. S. (1995). *Caminemos con Jesús: Toward a Hispanic/Latino theology of accompaniment*. New York: Orbis Book.

Goleman, D. (1995). *Emotional intelligence*. New York: Bantam Book.

Goleman, D., Boyatzis, R., & McKee, A. (2002). *Primal leadership*: Realizing the power of emotional intelligence. Boston: Harvard Business School.

Gouillart, F. J., & Kelly, J. N. (1995). *Building individual learning*. New York: McGraw-Hill.

Hall, C. C., Lindzey, G., & Campbell, J. B. (1998). *Theories of personality*. New York: John Wiley & Sons.

Hall, C.C., & Lindzey, G. (1978). *Theories of personality*. New York: John Wiley & Sons.

Haslam, D. R., & Harris, S. M. (2004): Informed consent documents of marriage and family therapists in practice: A qualitative analysis. *The American Journal of Family Therapy, 32*(4), 359-374.

Henderson, J. G., & Hawthorne, R. D. (2000). *Transformative curriculum leadership*. Columbus, OH: Prentice-Hall.

Hickman, G. R. (1998). *Leading organizations: Leadership and the social imperative of organizations in the 21ˢᵗ century*. Thousand Oaks, CA: Sage Publications.

Iparraguirre, J. I. (1963). *Obras Completas de San Ignacio de Loyola*. Madrid, Spain: La BAC Editores.

Johnson, R. B. (1997). Examining the validity structure of qualitative research. *Education 118*, 282-292.

Kahn, E. (1999). A critique of non-directivity in the person-centered approach. *Journal of Humanistic Psychology, 39*(4), 94-110.

Krefting, L. (1991). Rigor in qualitative research: The assessment of trustworthiness. *The American Journal of Occupational Therapy, 45,* 214-222.

Ledeen, M. A. (1999). *Machiavelli on modern leadership*. New York: St. Martin's Press.

Lincoln, Y. S. & Guba, E. A. (1985). Naturalistic inquiry. Beverly Hills, CA: Sage Publications.

Lowney, C. (2003). *Heroic leadership: Best practices from a 450-year-old company that changed the world*. Chicago: Loyola University Press.

Machiavelli, N. (1995). *The prince and other political writings*. North Clareton, VT: Orion House.

Magister Institute. (2004-2009). *Magister Institute collected papers*.

Magister Institute. (2004-2009). *Foundation meetings*.

Magister Institute. (2005). *Goizueta's DVD: La Virgen, los pobres y Magister*.

Magister Institute. (2004-2009). *Members' reflections*.

McDonough, P. (1992). *Men astutely trained: A history of the Jesuits in the American century*. New York: The Free Press.

McDonough, P., & Bianchi, E. (2002). *Passionate uncertainty: Inside the American Jesuits*. Los Angeles: University of California Press.

Milinki, A. K. (1999). *Cases in qualitative research*. Los Angeles: Pyrezak Publishing.

Moustakas, C. (1994). *Phenomenological research methods*. London: Sage Publications.

Moustakas, C. (1990). *Heuristic research: Design, methodology, and applications*. London: Sage Publications.

Napier, R. W., & Gershenfeld, M. K. (2004). *Groups: Theory and experience*. Boston: Houghton Mifflin.

O'Hara, M. (1995). Comment on Carl Rogers' "Toward a more human science of the person." *Journal of Humanistic Psychology, 25*(4), 25-30.

O'Neil, J. (1996). On emotional intelligence: a conversation with Daniel Goleman. *Educational Leadership, 54*(1), 6-11.

Patton, M. (2002). *Qualitative research and evaluation methods.* Thousand Oaks, CA: Sage.

Portes, A., & Bach, R. (1985). *Latin journey: Cuban and Mexican immigrants in the United States.* Berkeley, CA: University of California Press.

Quinn, R. (1993). Confronting Carl Rogers: A developmental interactional approach to person-centered therapy. *Journal of Humanistic Psychology, 33*(1), 6-23.

Roberts, J. M. (1993). *A short history of the world.* New York: Oxford University Press.

Rogers, C. R. (1942). *Counseling and psychotherapy.* Boston: Houghton Mifflin.

Rogers, C. R. (1951). *Client-centered therapy.* Boston, Houghton Mifflin.

Rogers, C. R., & Skinner, B. F. (1956). Some issues concerning the control of human behavior: A symposium. *Science, 124,* 1057-1066.

Rogers, C. R. (1961). *On becoming a person.* Boston: Houghton Mifflin.

Rogers, C. R., & Kinget, G. M. (1967). *Psicoterapia y relaciones humanas.* Madrid, Spain: Alfaguara.

Rogers, C. R. (1969). *Freedom to learn.* Columbus, OH: Charles E. Merrill Publishing.

Rogers, C. R. (1970). *Carl Rogers on encounter groups.* New York: Harper & Row Publishers.

Rogers, C. R. (1977). *Carl Rogers on personal power.* New York: Delacorte Press.

Rogers, C. R. (1985). Toward a more human science of the person. *Journal of Humanistic Psychology, 25*(4), 7-24.

Rosenau, P. M. (1992). *Post-modernism and the social sciences.* Princeton, NJ: Princeton University Press.

Rychlak, J. F. (1981). *Introduction to personality and psychotherapy.* Boston: Houghton Mifflin.

Saez, J. L. (1988). *Los Jesuitas en la Republica Dominicana* (Vol. I). Santo Domingo, DR: Museo Nacional de Historia y Geografia.

Saez, J. L.(1995). *Los Jesuitas en la Republica Dominicana* (Vol. II). Santo Domingo, DR: Museo Nacional de Historia y Gegrafia.

MAGISTER: THE PHENOMENON OF MISSION AND
CAMARADERIE ROGERS-FREIRE FOR SOCIAL JUSTICE.

153

San Juan Cafferty, P., & McCready, W. (1992). *Hispanics in the United States*. New Brunswick, NJ: Transaction Publishers.

Slife, B. D., & Williams, R. N. (1995). *What's behind the research?* Thousand Oaks, CA: Sage Publications.

Solomon, L. N. (1987). International tension-reduction through the person-centered approach. *Journal of Humanistic Psychology, 27*(3), 337-347.

Strauss, A., & Corbin, J. (1998). *Basics of qualitative research*. Thousand Oaks, CA: Sage Publications.

Swenson, G. L. (1987). When personal and political processes meet: The Rust Workshop. *Journal of Humanistic Psychology, 27*(3), 309-332.

Van Manen, M. (1990). *Researching lived experiences*. Ontario, Canada: The Althouse Press.

Yin, R. K. (2003). *Case study research: Design and methods*. Thousand Oaks, CA: Sage Publications.

Zucker, A. (1996). *Introduction to the philosophy of science*. Upper Saddle River, NJ: Prentice-Hall.

APPENDIX A

Magister Institute

The Executive Committee of the Magister Institute grants the necessary permissions to the Research conducted under the direction of Jose R. Cruz entitled: **Issues of Leadership from the Perspective of Former Jesuits: A Phenomenological Study.**

Cruz has been granted access to the information kept in our archives:

Magister Institute. (2004-2009). *Magister Institute collected papers.*

Magister Institute. (2004-2009). *Foundation meetings.*

Magister Institute. (2005). *Goizueta's DVD: La Virgen, los pobres y Magister.*

Magister Institute. (2004-2009). *Members' reflections.*

Jose R. Cruz has been our General Coordinator since our foundation.

Jose R. Cruz
Coordinador General
May 14, 2009

Jose Pedro Redondo, Ph.D.
Coordinador de Apostolado
May 14, 2009

APPENDIX B

Barry University
Informed Consent Form

Your participation in a research project is requested. The title of the study is

ISSUES OF LEADERSHIP FROM THE PERSPECTIVE OF FORMER JESUITS: A PHENOMENOLOGICAL STUDY

This research is being conducted by Jose R. Cruz, a doctoral student in the Leadership and Education department at Barry University, who is seeking information useful in the field of Leadership and Education. The aims of the research are to study the impact of the leadership strategies and other group processes in the creation and development of the Magister Institute.

As participants, you will be asked about your perceptions and experiences in the creation and development of the Magister Institute.

If you decide to participate in this research, you will be interviewed for a period of forty-five minutes to one hour. The interviews will be audiotaped and transcribed by this researcher. Following transcription of the transcripts, this researcher will invite you to review the information in the transcripts for collaboration and clarification purposes. Your time commitment is anticipated to be no more than 2 hours in total. Only this researcher will listen, transcribe, read and analyze the interviews. It is anticipated that there will be 5 former Jesuit participants in this study. Two Jesuit Priests familiar with the Magister Institute will also be interviewed for their perceptions on the process of developing this organization.

Your consent to be a research participant is strictly voluntary and should you decline to participate or choose to drop out at any time during the study, there will be no adverse effects. Should you withdraw from the study, any data collected from you will not be included in this study. This also includes that your refusal to participate at any point will have no impact on the personal or professional relationship with the researcher.

There are no anticipated risks of involvement in this study. Although there are no direct benefits to you, your participation in this study may help the understanding of the formation and creation of the Magister Institute. As a research participant, information you provide will be held in confidence to the extent permitted by law. Any published results of the research will refer to group averages only and no names will be used in the study. To safeguard your identities, the researcher will assign pseudonyms to participants; signed informed consent forms will be kept separate from the data and stored in separate locked file cabinets in this researcher's home office. The audiotape of the interview will be kept in separate storage under lock and key. All data, including transcripts, tapes and consent forms will be destroyed after five years.

If you have any questions or concerns regarding the study or your participation in the study, you may contact me, Jose R. Cruz at 786-236-8131, my supervisor Sister Phyllis Superfisky, SFCC, Ph.D. at (305)899-4835 or the Institutional Review Board point of contact, Barbara Cook, at (305)899-3020. If you are satisfied with the information provided and are willing to participate in this research, please signify your consent by signing this consent form.

Voluntary Consent

   I acknowledge that I have been informed of the nature and purposes of this experiment by ___Jose R. Cruz___ and that I have read and understand the information presented above, and that I have received a copy of this form for my records. I give my voluntary consent to participate in this experiment.

_____   _____

Signature of Participant   *Date*

_____   _____

Researcher   *Date*

APPENDIX C

Barry University
Informed Consent Form

(Current Jesuits)

Your participation in a research project is requested. The title of the study is

ISSUES OF LEADERSHIP FROM THE PERSPECTIVE OF FORMER JESUITS: A PHENOMENOLOGICAL STUDY

This research is being conducted <u>by Jose R. Cruz</u>, a doctoral student in the Leadership and Education department at Barry University, who is seeking information useful in the field of Leadership and Education. The aims of the research are to study the impact of the leadership strategies and other group processes in the creation and development of the Magister Institute.

As participants, you will be asked about your perceptions and experiences in the creation and development of the Magister Institute.

If you decide to participate in this research, you will be interviewed for a period of ten to twenty minutes. The interviews will be audiotaped and transcribed by this researcher. Following transcription of the transcripts, this researcher will invite you to review the information in the transcripts for collaboration and clarification purposes. Your time commitment is anticipated to be no more than 2 hours in total. Only this researcher will listen, transcribe, read and analyze the interviews. It is anticipated that there will be 5 former Jesuit participants in this study.

You, one of two Jesuit priests familiar with the Magister Institute will also be interviewed for your perceptions on the process of developing this organization

Your consent to be a research participant is strictly voluntary and should you decline to participate or choose to drop out at any time during the study, there will be no adverse effects. Should you withdraw from the study, any data collected from you will not be included in this study. This also includes that your refusal to participate at any point will have no impact on the personal or professional relationship with the researcher.

There are no anticipated risks of involvement in this study. Although there are no direct benefits to you, your participation in this study may help the understanding of the formation and creation of the Magister Institute and similar groups of former religious men and women in search for association or collaboration with the apostolic activities of religious organizations, parishes, and communities. As a research participant, information you provide will be held in confidence to the extent permitted by law. Any published results of the research will refer to group averages only and no names will be used in the study. To safeguard your identities, the researcher will assign pseudonyms to participants; signed informed consent forms will be kept separate from the data and stored in separate locked file cabinets in this researcher's home office. The audiotape of the interview will be kept in separate storage under lock and key. All data, including transcripts, tapes and consent forms will be destroyed after five years.

If you have any questions or concerns regarding the study or your participation in the study, you may contact me, Jose R. Cruz at 786-236-8131, my supervisor Sister Phyllis Superfisky, SFCC, Ph.D. at (305)899-4835 or the Institutional Review Board point of contact, Barbara Cook, at (305)899-3020. If you are satisfied with the information provided and are willing to participate in this research, please signify your consent by signing this consent form. Voluntary Consent

I acknowledge that I have been informed of the nature and purposes of this experiment by Jose R. Cruz   and that I have read and understand the information presented above, and that I have received a copy of this form for my records. I give my voluntary consent to participate in this experiment.

_____   _____

Signature of Participant   *Date*

_____   _____

Researcher   *Date*

APPENDIX D

Interview Questions

The general overarching research questions are the following:

What are your recollections/perceptions of your lived experiences in the creation and development of the Magister Institute?

What are your recollections/ perceptions of the leadership style of the Executive Committee in the creation and development of the Magister Institute?

The following five research subquestions are presented as a stimulus and inspiration to help each research participant accurately describe a more comprehensive depiction of the phenomenon under scrutiny from their personal point of view or frame of reference.

1.1 What, in your own words, are all the aspects of your feelings of separation from the Society of Jesus, as well as the experiences you have encountered with the religious and lay administrations of the Catholic Church?

1.2. What were the leadership strategies and any other ideas, feelings or emotions connected with the Society of Jesus that you consider most influential in the consolidation of the Magister Institute?

1.3. What were your fears and hopes for re-association with the Jesuits? What connection do you see between the leadership style of the Executive Committee and the reduction of your fears?

1.4. With the degree of success attained in the re-association of the former Jesuits of the Magister Institute with the current Jesuits in the Antilles Province, how much of this accomplishment do you think is related to the leadership style of members of the Magister Institute?

MAGISTER: THE PHENOMENON OF MISSION AND
CAMARADERIE ROGERS-FREIRE FOR SOCIAL JUSTICE.

163

1.5. What do you think are the possibilities of success of similar alternatives elsewhere in the Catholic Church? Given your experience at the Magister Institute, and the scarcity of Jesuits, what do you think of the interest shown by the Society of Jesus in re-associating with the former Jesuits to provide apostolic work? What are your thoughts about the degree and kind of re-association achieved between the current Jesuits of Miami, Florida, U.S.A., Dominican Republic, and Cuba, called the Antilles Province of the Society of Jesus, and the former Jesuits of the Magister Institute?

APPENDIX E

Guide of Procedures for Analysis of Data

1. Gathering all data from one research participant. The initial step of the organizing, handling, and synthesis-producing process is gathering all data from one research participant. This includes the taped interviews, the depictions, any notes about the participants, and any document related to this research participant.

2. Immersion. This material is studied and analyzed, until it is thoroughly understood.

3. The first draft of the depiction. Here a period of rest is followed by one of intense study and analysis. Then codification and theme production is intensified. The first draft of the depiction is constructed. The language and the examples of the depiction are all from the individual research participant's experience of the phenomenon.

4. Back to the data to find congruence between the depictions already constructed. In case the raw data backs the description and the details selected from the depiction, the first case is temporarily finished.

5. Full revision. In the event that questions are raised and more time is required to fix the discrepancies found, a full revision is accommodated.

6. The second case or research participant is undertaken following the same course of organization (Moustakas, 1990) and analysis follows. This second case will be ended with an individual depiction responding to the data gathered for the second research participant.

7. The depictions are ready. All individual descriptions are gathered together and reviewed following a systematic procedure: the main researcher proceeds to go intensely into the entire group of depictions then takes each one until he considers all parts (themes) of the

phenomenon as described in these depictions are understood and made a part of him. Here the commonalities and the idiosyncrasies are identified and assimilated by the researcher.

8. The first group-depiction of commonalities and idiosyncrasies is developed. This depiction provides examples of descriptive accounts, narratives, conversations, illustrations, and other examples that help reproduce the lively and dynamic spirit of the phenomenon.

9. The next step consists in creating a common and most representative depiction of the entire group, by first using examples of the union of those depictions that best represent the entire group.

10. Finally, the researcher repeats the entire process and develops a fitting synthesis of the phenomenon. This final depiction is a product of study and analysis systematically carried out, but it is also a synthesis developed by the one most immersed in the depictions and responsible for the synthetic rendition of the individual and group depictions (Moustakas, 1990).

APPENDIX F

GRAPH OF QUOTATIONS BY PERSONS AND THEMES

First Set of Quotations

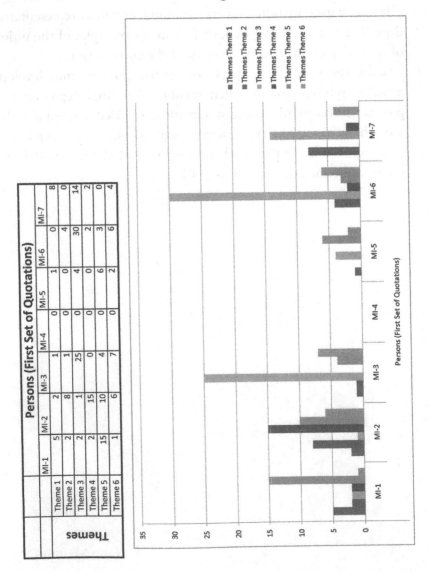

Persons (First Set of Quotations)							
	MI-1	MI-2	MI-3	MI-4	MI-5	MI-6	MI-7
Theme 1	5	2	2	1	0	1	0	8
Theme 2	2	8	1	1	0	0	4	0
Theme 3	2	1	25	0	0	4	30	14
Theme 4	2	15	0	0	0	0	2	2
Theme 5	15	10	4	0	0	6	3	0
Theme 6	1	6	7	0	0	2	6	4

APPENDIX G

GRAPH OF QUOTATIONS BY PERSONS AND THEMES

Second Set of Quotations

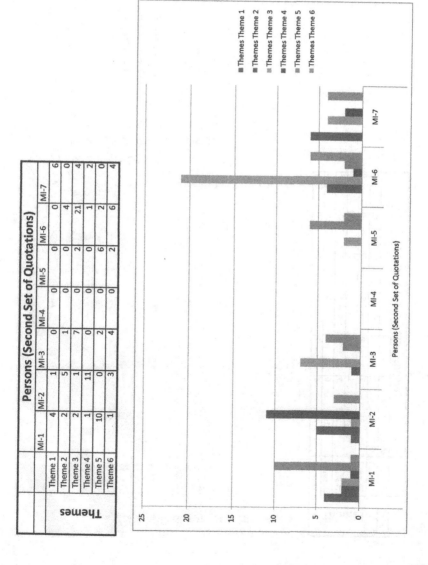

		MI-1	MI-2	MI-3	MI-4	MI-5	MI-6	MI-7
Themes	Theme 1	4	4	1	0	0	0	6
	Theme 2	2	5	1	0	4	0	0
	Theme 3	2	1	7	2	21	4	4
	Theme 4	1	11	0	0	1	0	2
	Theme 5	10	0	2	6	2	0	0
	Theme 6	1	3	4	2	6	4	4

Persons (Second Set of Quotations)

APPENDIX H

GRAPH OF QUOTATIONS BY PERSONS AND THEMES

Last Set of Quotations

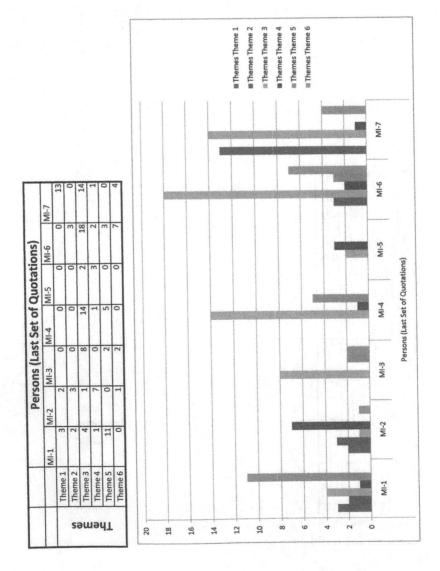

Persons (Last Set of Quotations)

Themes	MI-1	MI-2	MI-3	MI-4	MI-5	MI-6	MI-7
Theme 1	3	2	0	0	0	0	13
Theme 2	2	3	0	0	0	3	0
Theme 3	4	1	8	14	2	18	14
Theme 4	1	7	0	1	3	2	1
Theme 5	11	0	2	5	0	3	0
Theme 6	0	1	2	0	0	7	4

APPENDIX I

CURRICULUM VITAE

Jose R. Cruz

Address: 7420 SW Sunset Drive, Miami, FL 3314
Phone: 305/ 667-2722 (H)
305/ 445-7876 (School)
786-236-8131 (Cell)

WORK EXPERIENCE:
Current Position:

Guidance Counselor
Coconut Grove Elementary, Miami, Florida

EDUCATION:

A.B. - Spring Hill College, Mobile, Alabama
(Philosophy and Mathematics)

M.Ed. (GPA: 3.5) Loyola University of Chicago
(Guidance and Counseling); completed the four
year program from the Bellarmine School of
Theology of Chicago (four years of Theology),
was ordained a Priest at Gesu Church in Miami,
and worked as a Jesuit Priest for nine years.

Doctoral Studies
Loyola University of Chicago (42 Semester
Hours in Psychology equivalent to Specialist in
Guidance and Counseling)
(GPA: 3.8) at Florida International University in
Community College Teaching.

Ph.D. Program: Educational Leadership
Barry University (GPA: 3.9) in Educational
Leadership (Comprehensive Exams passed in
October, 2005)
Current Professional Educator's Certificate
Educational Leadership, Guidance and
Counseling.

WORK EXPERIENCE

Elementary-Middle-High School Level Administration

Principal   Loyola School, Miami
                             Santa Barbara High School, Santo Domingo

Assistant Principal   Jose de Diego Middle School, Miami, (M-DCPS)
                             Silver Bluff Elementary School, Miami
                             (M-DCPS)
                             Colegio Loyola, Santo Domingo (Jesuit High
                             School)

College Level Administration

Rector/President and Dean   World University of Santo **Domingo** (3
                                 years as Rector and Dean of Graduate Studies)

Director   Master's Program in Community Psychology at
                             UASD   State University of Santo Domingo
                             (3 years)
                             Department of Psychology (3 years) at UNPHU
                             National University of Santo Domingo
                             Administrative Services (2 years) at the Miami
                             Institute of Psychology (Carlos Albizu University
                             today).

National Level Administration

> National Director of Mental Health of the
> Dominican Republic (3 years)
> National Illiteracy Campaign of the Dominican
> Republic

Teaching and Counseling Guidance Counselor at Citrus Grove Middle;
Counselor at Allapattah Middle (8 years); teacher
of Mathematics in different private schools (3
years); teacher of Psychology at several Colleges
and Universities including the Miami Institute of
Psychology (15 years). Professor of Psychology of
Religious Experience and of Psychology and Faith
for three years at Loyola University of Chicago.

Coaching and Athletic Director

> Athletic Director and Commissioner in several
> high schools and clubs; basketball and baseball
> coach in middle schools and athletic clubs in
> Miami.

OTHER EXPERIENCES MAC SCHOOL SCHEDULE BUILDING
Department of Technological Training of
MDCPS.

Former Director

> Xavier Center (Christian Life Community) in
> Santo Domingo

Founder and Director Casa Abierta, a psychological and prevention
center Archdiocese of Santo Domingo El Rincon
Community Center, a drug addiction clinic
Archdiocese of Chicago, Illinois

Director   Dare Program of the Archdiocese of Miami

Religion Teacher   Loyola School, Santo Domingo
                                Columbus High School, Miami.
                                Joliet Academy (Catholic) School in Illinois
                                Loyola University of Chicago
                                Permanent Deacons Program in Chicago

Christian Life Community (CVX)
                                Former General Coordinator of Magister
                                Institute, Affiliated (CVX) to the Archdiocese
                                of Miami and to the Society of Jesus.

BOOKS WRITTEN   *Towards Personality Development*
                                (College textbook in Guidance and Counseling
                                for high schools)

                                A Psychology for the Young Dominican
                                (High school textbook in psychology)

                                Religion and youth in Latin America. A comparison
                                study of youth in Caracas and Santo Domingo.

PROFESSIONAL PAPERS
                                Juvenile delinquency today: Analysis and suggestions.
                                Presented at the Regional Symposium on Juvenile
                                Delinquency, Universidad Nordestana, San
                                Francisco de Macoris, D.R., January, 1985.

                                *Notes about the future of psychology in the
                                Dominican Republic.* National Congress of
                                Psychology, organized by the Dominican
                                Association of Psychology (ADOPSI), Santo
                                Domingo, D.R., June 2, 1984.

Juvenile Gangs (with Ramos, C., Belliard, L., &
Gonzalez, F.). National Congress of Psycholgy,
organized by ADOPSI, Santo Domingo, D.R.,
May 14, 1983.

A master's degree in community psychology. American
Psychological Association, 90th Annual Convention,
August 23-27, 1982, Washington, DC.

*College Teaching: some modifications to the Rogerian
method.* National Congress of Psycholgy,
organized by ADOPSI, Santo Domingo, D.R.,
Aprol 3, 1982.

*Contributions of Community Psychology to drug
preventive education.* Organized by Casa Abierta,
Archdiocese of Santo Domingo, National Public
Library, 1981.

*The Licentia and Master's programs of psychology
in Santo Domingo, D.R.* First Latin American
Seminar on the teaching of psychology (college
level). Organized by the Universidad Central de
Venezuela, Caracas, 1981.

From Rogers to Freire: Part II. International
Congress of Psychology, organized by the
Interamerican Psychological Association (SIP),
Santo Domingo, D.R., June 25, 1981.

From Rogers to Freire: I. A national seminar on
contemporary psychology. Organized by the
Department of Psychology of UASD, Santo
Domingo, D.R., 1981.

Social Role of the professional psychology in Santo Domingo. Seminar organized by the Department of Psychology of the State University of Santo Domingo (UASD), November 26, 1980.

The master's program in community psychology at the State University of Santo Domingo. Symposium organized by ADOPSI in recognition of the development of community psychology in the D.R. and the contributions made by Jose R. Cruz. National Public Library, October 15, 1980.

A new role for the community psychologist. International Congress of Community Psychology. Havana, September 1979.

Rappaport: a critical appraisal. International Congress of Community Psycholgy. Havana, September, 1979.

The foundation of the department of Psychology of the National University Pedro Henriquez Urena (UNPHU): 1967-1969. Organized by ADOPSI as an act of recognition to Jose R. Cruz its first director and founder. National Public Library, October 20, 1977.

Drug rehabilitation techniques for Santo Domingo. Symposium of the half-way house concept of re-education. Organized by Casa Abierta of the Archdiocese of Santo Domingo, June, 1977.

Techniques and therapeutic style of Casa Abierta, Archdiocese of Santo Domingo. Organized by the First National Congress of Psychiatry of the D.R, 1976.

The moral judgment of the child according to Jean Piaget. Published by: Revista Casa Abierta, II, 2, 1976, 28-32.

Sexuality and Personality, I, II, and III. In Revista Casa Abierta, II, June 1975, 21-29.

Drug Addiction and coercive education. Published in El Sol, Santo Domingo, May 13 and 14, 1974.

The Latins and the Americans: a comparative essay. Professional presentation at the Symposium of the department of philosophy of Loyola University of Chicago, September 1970. Published by the Chicago Sun-Times, January 5, 1971.

Towards a psychology of the young Dominican. In the Symposium of psychosocial studies, Santo Domingo High School of the Adrian Dominican Sisters. Published in Estudios Sociales, II, 3, 1969, 143-147.

Printed in the United States
By Bookmasters